FOREVER EVERTON!

FOREVER EVERTON!

THIRTY-FIVE YEARS OF TRIUMPHS AND TRIALS

STAN LIVERSEDGE

Foreword by JOE ROYLE

MAINSTREAM PUBLISHING

EDINBURGH AND LONDON

First published in 1995 by
MAINSTREAM PUBLISHING COMPANY (EDINBURGH) LTD
7 Albany Street
Edinburgh EH1 3UG

ISBN 1 85158 813 2

Photographs courtesy of John Cocks, *Bootle Times Herald*, *Liverpool Daily
Post & Echo*, and *Mersey Soccer*

A catalogue record for this book is available from the British Library

Typeset in 11 on 13 pt Caslon
Printed and bound in Great Britain by Butler & Tanner Ltd, Frome

Contents

FOREVER EVERTON!

One for all, all for one,
We're forever Everton!
We're up for the League,
We're up for the Cup,
Everton's on the up and up!
EVERTON! EVERTON! EVERTON!
We're forever EVERTON!

Author's Note

I should like to express my thanks to Joe Royle for agreeing to contribute a Foreword to this book, and to Everton Football Club for their co-operation concerning the photographs. While the book generally records the events spanning some 35 years, I have taken the liberty of including many of my personal recollections – and, of course, expressing my own views on various matters, in so far as they affected me.

Foreword by

JOE ROYLE

It did not take me more than a few seconds to give my answer when I was asked if I would return to Goodison Park as Everton's manager. In a word, the answer was 'Yes' – coupled with a question of my own: 'When do you want me to start?' And so, suddenly, in November 1994, my career in football took a new turning while, at the same time, going back along an old, familiar road, as I retraced my steps to Goodison Park.

Back in 1972, when I was still an Everton footballer, the players at the club made a record, and the ditty is still sung today. The title: *Forever Everton!*. And you'll see the first verse of this song on another page. For me, it remains very appropriate, because the Blues were my first love in football, and although I travelled on, when my days as a player at Goodison Park had come to an end, I never foreswore the allegiance I owed to Everton Football Club. I know, of course, that I am like many others; we call ourselves Everton fans. When I was asked to return, this time as manager, I didn't even wait to find out the terms of the contract – which should demonstrate clearly enough the depth of feeling I have always had for this great club.

When I first pulled on the royal-blue jersey, I was a teenager filled with hope and ambition, and during the late 1960s I was fortunate enough to share in the club's successes. Now, as Everton's manager, I have a different responsibility, in that it's my job to produce a team which can take the club forward and build upon our success in the FA Cup and the Charity Shield.

I realise full well that it will be no easy job; but I believe I have learned my managerial trade over a dozen years (and discovered many of its pitfalls, as well). As this book demonstrates, football isn't always a game where the going is easy, and Everton have had both good and bad times during the past 35 years. I experienced some of those ups and downs during my career as a player at Goodison Park and, of course, I have many personal recollections of events and personalities there.

One thing I can say without hesitation: this club has never ceased to aspire to greatness. The aim has always been to be up there with the finest in the land. Not for nothing is the club motto *Nil Satis Nisi Optimum*: and that means 'Nothing but the Best'. Of course, I cannot give any guarantee about results; but I do guarantee that so long as I am manager of this great club, we shall not fail for the want of trying. And I am well aware that, right through the pages of *Forever Everton!*, the underlying theme is one which relates to a club that constantly seeks success, not least for the fans who follow it so loyally.

Chapter One

AN AFFAIR OF THE HEART

Joe Royle achieved, in a matter of a few months, something which Graeme Souness, during the best part of three years, never quite managed to do – he got the backing of the Liverpool fraternity on Merseyside in full – although it has to be admitted that this was largely because Everton had put the skids under Manchester United in the final of the FA Cup. And for the fans who normally flock to Anfield, this was almost as good as seeing their own favourites give Alex Ferguson's team a beating.

Souness ended his reign at Liverpool amid the kind of controversy which had surrounded his career as manager; and when he quit, it was recorded that 'people power' had brought about his downfall (not to mention the débâcle of an FA Cup exit at the hands of unfashionable Bristol City). It was 'people power' which played a significant part, also, in the emergence of Joe Royle as Everton's FA Cup-winning manager in the spring of 1995, after the previous incumbent of the hot seat at Goodison Park, Mike Walker, had succumbed to the pressures of the job.

Over a period of months, Walker had succeeded in one thing: if results hadn't gone his way, he had survived by the skin of his teeth – but, as relegation stared Everton in the face for the second season on the trot, and the fans became bitterly disenchanted with the state of affairs at their club, chairman Peter Johnson decided the time had come to pull the plug, and Mike Walker became Everton's ex-manager, thus following in the footsteps of Howard Kendall and Colin Harvey before him. Both Harvey and Kendall had been team-mates of Joe Royle during some of Everton's glory years.

If the 1960s had belonged to Everton and Liverpool the 1980s were dominated once again by Merseyside's Big Two as, between them, Everton and Liverpool collected the lion's share of the major trophies, both on the domestic scene and in competition with the Continentals. The Championship, for instance, went to Howard Kendall's team twice in the mid-1980s, with Liverpool sandwiching the classic League–FA Cup double in between. Liverpool had finished as top dogs three seasons in succession, from 1981–82 to 1983–84 and, of course, they had claimed the European Cup and the Milk Cup.

But they were taken to a replay in the final of the Milk Cup against Everton in 1984 before Graeme Souness drilled home the only goal; and Everton collected the European Cup–Winners Cup in season 1984–85 (they beat Rapid Vienna 3–1 in Rotterdam), after Liverpool had won the Champions Cup in 1981 and 1984, and gone to the ill-fated final of 1985 (which ended with English clubs bowing out of European competition, following the Heysel Stadium disaster). That period of exile effectively prevented Everton from trying their luck in the Champions Cup after they had claimed the League title in the spring of 1985, when Liverpool were runners-up, just as Everton came second when their rivals won back the trophy in 1986. Then, in 1987, it was Everton first and Liverpool second again.

Howard Kendall certainly had his headaches during season 1986–87, because he had to call upon no fewer than 23 players – only one of whom (Kevin Ratcliffe) was able to play in every League game. Injuries affected almost every position; yet Everton hit the top in February and (apart from slipping to second place in the middle of March) held on, winning ten of their last dozen matches. Oddly enough, they had parted with the man who, the previous term, had struck 30 goals for them in 41 League appearances . . . yet this still hadn't brought them the title trophy. The player: Gary Lineker, signed from Leicester City in July 1985 for a club-record fee of £800,000 and sold on to Barcelona just 12 months later for a cool £2.75 million. Lineker succeeded team-mate Neville Southall in 1986 as Footballer of the Year. When Everton signed Lineker, they agreed to pay a percentage of any future transfer fee if the player was sold within two years, so Leicester benefited from the £2.75 million bonanza as well. In the 1986 FA Cup final Lineker scored Everton's goal – but Liverpool struck three times, to achieve the double. Yes, those were heady days for the fans of both Merseyside clubs.

For a while, indeed, Howard Kendall was lauded as the manager who had brought back the good times to Goodison; then, when he departed for sunny Spain and the challenge of a job with Athletic Bilbao, Colin Harvey stepped into the breach. However, the time came when results dictated a change of manager and Kendall (by this time steering Manchester City towards safety) returned, with Harvey reverting to a role on the coaching side. Ironically, Harvey was to join Oldham later as the second-in-command to Graeme Sharp – who had been signed from Everton by Joe Royle and who became Royle's successor at Boundary Park.

At the time he left Maine Road, Kendall described his job with City as having been like a love affair, while the attraction of returning to Everton was likened to the bond of a marriage. The marriage foundered, and Walker arrived – not, it has to be admitted, with the unconfined blessing of his previous club, Norwich City, who complained to the powers-that-be and sought compensation for having lost their team boss to Everton. Then, while the fortunes of Norwich City fluctuated and faded, so did the fortunes of Mike Walker at Goodison Park, where his days became numbered after the arrival of Peter Johnson. There was further irony in the fact that Johnson, a wealthy man (reputed to be even wealthier than Liverpool chairman David Moores), had been regarded as a Liverpool fan. But with the Moores family shareholding in Everton said to be up for grabs, Johnson assumed control after a boardroom takeover battle which had involved impresario Bill Kenwright, once of *Coronation Street* and noted also as an Everton supporter. Any hatchets there might have been were well and truly buried as the task of resurrecting Everton's dipping fortunes began anew.

If Peter Johnson had been touted as a Liverpool fan, Joe Royle had always struck me as a fellow who would rarely go to Anfield to watch Liverpool – not purely for pleasure, anyway. Throughout his life he had been a dyed-in-the-wool, true-blue Evertonian – even if he had once talked to Bill Shankly about joining Liverpool. Come to that, Royle could have become a Busby Babe; he certainly had the opportunity, had he been of a mind to sign for Manchester United. But after considering his options, he put pen to paper for Everton. He didn't always have it easy as a player, though, and as a manager he faced some tough problems trying to achieve success at Oldham on a shoestring.

When Everton sacked Mike Walker and installed Joe Royle as manager, the soccer wheel had turned full circle for the lad from Norris Green. He had gone from a terraced house – No. 24 Parkhurst Road – to accommodation which was considerably more salubrious, up on the moors above Oldham (a residence which had been converted from a sanatorium), and in footballing terms he had enjoyed visits to Wembley, as well as international recognition. But he had come to the sad conclusion that his chance of returning to manage the Goodison Park club had vanished – the arrival of Mike Walker seemed to confirm this.

Royle had seen Howard Kendall come and go; he had seen Colin Harvey make way for Kendall again. And while the media indulged in its popular game of putting names in the frame, with Joe Royle's being given considerable publicity, the choice fell upon Norwich City's team boss, who had done an excellent job in a comparatively brief spell at Carrow Road. The decision by Everton to appoint Walker appeared to spell the end of Royle's dreams. Once again, despite the fact that he had been tipped to take over at Everton, it just hadn't happened for Joe Royle; and so he soldiered on at homely Oldham.

Then, virtually overnight, the situation changed with dramatic impact. Joe Royle was asked to return to the club to which he had given his unswerving allegiance since his teenage days – days when, as a strapping and still-growing giant of sixteen, he was pitched into Everton's first team. It was a shock promotion, to say the least, and it began and ended amid great controversy as Everton lost at Blackpool and manager Harry Catterick found himself being abused and attacked by irate fans. For Royle, it was a salutary experience; but although he went back to the comparative obscurity of the reserves for a spell, he did bounce back and thus repaid Catterick's faith in him. Indeed, he became one of the heroes in a team which produced such flowing football that the supporters labelled Everton the School of Soccer Science. That was in the era of the Swinging Sixties, when Everton had a galaxy of footballing talent and they were a match for any side in the land.

There were international players throughout Everton's side: Gordon West of England in goal; Scots such as Bobby Collins, Alex Parker, Alex Scott and Alex Young. The last-named was a centre-forward whom the fans adored – they called the flaxen-haired Young 'the Golden Vision', and he displayed some of the silkiest touches in the game. With winger Scott supplying a service, and the incisive finishing of Welsh international Roy Vernon, Everton were a team well worth watching. As for their defence, during the later part of the 1960s they had the rock-like England international Brian Labone at centre-half, along with World Cup medal-winners

Ramon Wilson and Alan Ball, and others besides.

At the start of the 1960s, Joe Royle was still merely dreaming of footballing fame – he had to wait a few seasons before he broke through to Everton's first team. By the time he made it, Everton had won the League Championship (in season 1962–63), competed in the European Cup against Helenio Herrera's great Inter Milan side, claimed the FA Cup in a controversial final (1966) and were heading for their second title trophy, and a return to Wembley. Royle played for Everton in the 1968 final against West Bromwich Albion (for whom Jeff Astle struck the single-goal winner), and he figured in the Championship-winning side of season 1969–70.

In between the two title successes during Harry Catterick's management, Everton fans had seen the League honours go in turn to Liverpool, Manchester United, Liverpool again, Manchester United once more, Manchester City and Leeds United. When Everton won the FA Cup in May 1995 with Joe Royle as their manager – and after they had staved off relegation – they denied Manchester United even the consolation of retaining one trophy, just a year after United had done the double.

Soon after Joe joined Everton as an ambitious teenager, he began going out with a Merseyside girl by the name of Janet Hughes. When he became the youngest centre-forward in the English First Division, he was earning good money – enough to take Janet out and treat her to a nice meal, enough to splash out £750 on a British racing-green TR4 car, enough to buy two or three thirty-guinea suits at a time, if he were in the mood to do so. He was 19 years old and labelled a teenage tycoon.

Young as he was, though, he had the savvy to realise that he wouldn't be able to play top-class football all his life, and that the good times must come to an end; so he took out an insurance policy which would provide him with what people term 'a nest-egg' by the time he had reached the age of 40.

By the spring of 1995, Joe Royle was 45 – and by then, also, Janet had been his wife for a considerable time. Indeed, when Joe and Jan visited Adelaide, in South Australia, during the summer of 1995, they were celebrating their silver wedding.

By that time, too, Joe was still in partnership with his long-time buddy, Willie Donachie, a former Scotland international who was capped more than 30 times, and who rarely offers two words when he thinks one will suffice. Joe and Willie have been soccer nomads over the years, although the game has been good to them. Joe left Everton and played on, for Manchester City (he won a medal with them), Bristol City and Norwich City; Willie left Manchester City after having given them sterling service over many years, enjoyed a spell with Portland Timbers in the North American Soccer League, then returned to England and fetched up at Burnley, before teaming up with Joe Royle at Oldham Athletic, where he coached and carried on playing until he was coming up to the age of 40. Even then, he could still show the youngsters a thing or two.

Between them, Joe Royle and Willie Donachie got through the tough times and gave Oldham Athletic not just respectability and a brief spell in the Premier League; they also resurrected the fortunes of footballers whose careers, to say the least, appeared to have been put on hold. In the process, Oldham Athletic were able to make millions of pounds on transfer deals – indeed, Joe Royle became the Man with the Midas Touch, as he signed players for peanuts (or even on free transfers) and sold them for small fortunes. Along the way, Oldham profited from deals with clubs such as Leeds United and Manchester City to a degree where it became embarrassing in view of the bargains they got. Things reached a stage where Royle became almost afraid to ring a club and ask about a player, so deftly had he done his job of buying, then selling at a profit.

The names of the bargain buys and free-transfer

acquisitions are quite astonishing: Denis Irwin, Paul Warhurst, Earl Barrett, Andy Goram, Andy Linighan, Andy Ritchie, Tommy Wright, Mark Ward, John Ryan, Mike Milligan, Rick Holden, Ian Marshall, Neil Adams . . . When Joe Royle – of sheer necessity – went shopping in soccer's bargain basement, he did it supremely well. And after he had taken charge of team affairs at Everton in November 1994 he was able to say, for the first time: 'Now we can go shopping at Harrods.' No more scouting around Woolies, as it were.

Not that it was rags to riches all the way, because only a few months before Royle finally landed the job of his dreams, Everton had been reportedly £4 million in the red, with the Moores family – generous Goodison benefactors for so many years – apparently wanting to unload their shareholding. By then, Sir John Moores was well into his 90s – he died at the age of 97 – and the club's future seemed to be shrouded in uncertainty. It was said, when Howard Kendall called it a day as Everton's manager, that he had quit after he learned that the club would not agree to let him spend £1.5 million on Manchester United striker Dion Dublin.

In the meantime, Joe Royle had gone the whole hog for Oldham Athletic when he splashed half a million pounds on Everton striker Graeme Sharp (who succeeded him as Oldham's manager) and £750,000 on another striker, Ian Olney (whose career was dogged by injury, but whose goals during the final week of season 1992–93 helped to secure Oldham's survival in the Premiership, if only for another 12 months). Royle, in fact, during his time at Oldham, was saddled with the tremendous extra burden of unfair competition, in that he was expected to get the club competing with the likes of moneybags Manchester United, Liverpool and, yes, Everton. Oldham really had no right to be playing on the same pitch as Alex Ferguson's multi-millionaire assembly of players.

Yet Royle steered Oldham to two FA Cup semi-finals against Manchester United (they went desperately close to winning the second of these); he took Oldham into the First Division (they claimed the Second Division Championship with a penalty goal on the final day of the season); he took the Boundary Park club to the final of the Littlewoods Cup; and he saw his homespun side knock both Everton and Arsenal off the Wembley trail.

It was a bargain buy from Everton (Ian Marshall) who helped to do the damage against the Goodison Park club, while after Arsenal had taken a hammering at Boundary Park their then manager, George Graham, arrived in the tiny press room to declare that the defeat was 'an unacceptable result' for a club of the Gunners' stature, while at the same time giving Oldham full credit for their display. In another Cup-tie, against Scarborough, Frankie Bunn scored six goals for Oldham (his career then went on the downward slope, as injury struck); while in the first leg of their Littlewoods Cup semi-final against West Ham, Oldham as a collective unit hammered home half a dozen goals – and even then, the home fans felt that the return at Upton Park could be no formality.

In those heady days, Oldham still really needed to score four goals or more before their supporters could settle down and relax – and even then, as events proved, it could be touch and go. In the second leg, when they were trailing 3–0, it became an anxious time for Joe Royle and his men, although they got through. And on the final day of their first season in the Premier League, they had it all to do against Southampton, while still requiring Arsenal to score a victory over Crystal Palace at Highbury. When the Gunners went ahead, there was little doubt about the result of that match; but at Boundary Park, even though Oldham cruised into a 4–1 lead, hearts were still in mouths as the scoreline crept to 4–3 with minutes still to go. With the fans imploring the referee to blow his whistle, down on the bench Joe Royle and his backroom team were living on their nerves – but, at last, they got the result they sought.

An Affair of the Heart   21

A member of Oldham's backroom staff confided to me that three months previously he had confessed his fears about relegation to Joe Royle, only to be told, in confident fashion: 'Don't worry; we'll stay up.' Asked how he could be so sure, Oldham's manager replied: 'Because I'm a lucky bugger!' And when Oldham had indeed secured their safety, Joe Royle was moved to observe: 'There must surely be a place in the Premier League for a club like us.' What he meant was that Oldham – an attacking side – provided much-needed flair and excitement in a game so often played 'by numbers'. Before that crucial match against the Saints, he had simply instructed his troops to go for it. And they did.

In that final week, Oldham had gone to Villa Park and snuffed out the hopes Ron Atkinson had cherished of steering his expensive side to the Championship, while Liverpool manager Graeme Souness had seen his men suffer a mid-week defeat at Boundary Park. In a sense, Oldham handed the Championship to Alex Ferguson's Manchester United – who, after beating Oldham twice in FA Cup duels, were third-time unlucky when Joe Royle's Everton did their stuff at Wembley in 1995. That's how football fortunes can turn.

According to Alex Ferguson (who, so often, is pictured on television looking intense when United are in action), Joe Royle 'is one of those people who can handle pressure . . . he's always got a laugh and a joke, and doesn't take it too seriously'. Well, I have known Joe Royle since his teenage days, and I've seen him under pressure, as well as when he has savoured success. After a bad result, I've asked him: 'Have you got over it now?' Unfailingly, the answer has been: 'Of course I have – I'm okay. Why shouldn't I be?' Unlike Bill Shankly, Joe Royle doesn't believe that football is more important than life and death – although he does take his job very seriously; seriously enough, indeed, to the point where, now and again, he might well have considered packing in the job while he was managing Oldham. That would not have been surprising, considering how he was expected constantly to be working miracles; but he carried on and gained his reward by landing the job at Everton. Along the way, he also demonstrated tremendous loyalty to Oldham Athletic, the club which had first given him his chance in football management.

There was a brief moment when it was suggested that the job at West Ham could be Joe Royle's, and there were other occasions when – according to the media – his name was in the frame for other managerial posts. There was the much-publicised bid by Manchester City, also, to prise him away from Boundary Park. But as City sought to tempt him back to Maine Road, where he had enjoyed success as a player, the Oldham fans pleaded with him not to desert their club. Joe pondered . . . and decided to stay. After all, one of the things he had long preached to his players was that the grass wasn't always greener on the other side of the fence – as Mike Milligan discovered, when he joined Everton for close to a million pounds.

Milligan never really settled in at Goodison Park and, eventually, he returned to Oldham for a fee of £600,000. This was another shrewd stroke of business by Joe Royle who, before he left Boundary Park, sold Milligan on again, this time to one of Joe's former clubs, Norwich City, for £750,000. And, since Milly had been a home-grown player in the first place, Oldham could be well satisfied with the overall profit they had made.

Joe Royle hasn't always been everyone's favourite. He's had his brushes with players, and with some of the media men from the London area. Generally speaking, however, he can be relied upon to come face to face with the press after a match, no matter what the result, and – after he's accepted a can of beer to wet his whistle – he'll manage to produce a smile and a few pithy one-liners, even if they're sometimes of the rueful variety. I can recall an occasion when he referred to the chairman of a certain club as 'The Ayatollah'.

It wasn't said maliciously, but with gentle humour, as the name of this particular character cropped up during the course of conversation.

I've always found Joe Royle to be nothing, if not honest, too. He will do his utmost to keep club business to himself, and he's been very accommodating to the local paper when it comes to disseminating club news. At the start of season 1994–95, after Oldham had finally relinquished their hold on a place in the Premiership, I spoke to Joe about his and the club's future – not that I expected to be given chapter and verse. When I raised the question of reinforcements for the team, Joe – being candid as ever – told me (and not for the first time during his reign as Oldham's team boss) that 'we haven't a bean'. Once again, he was in the business of selling to make ends meet, although when Leeds United tried to buy defender Richard Jobson, a reported offer of around £1 million was turned down.

I suspect that later Joe Royle had some regrets about this, and for various reasons. 'Jobbo', never a moment's trouble so far as I know, had arrived at Boundary Park from Hull City as a £400,000 signing by Royle, and he had graduated to the status of being a member of the England international squad – his career had initially blossomed under Graham Taylor at Watford.

Maybe Joe felt that if he hung on Oldham would get more than a million for Richard Jobson; maybe he felt that if he allowed the player to go, it would open up the floodgates for transfer requests from others in his squad, after the bitter disappointment of relegation. Whatever the reason for the Leeds offer being rejected, it turned out badly for club and player. Jobson, who sustained an injury which kept him on the sidelines for many weary months, finally got the go-ahead to play again . . . by which time Leeds had come back with a revised bid of £800,000, plus more if things went well. However, just when it seemed that Jobson was being given a second chance and Oldham were going to collect, the medical verdict went against the player, so he had to remain at Boundary Park.

Meanwhile, it was Joe Royle who had moved on. The moment of truth had arrived for Oldham's manager, and when Everton had triumphed over Manchester United in the 1995 FA Cup final, there was a moving moment as Royle and Donachie embraced each other. Together, they had endured some difficult times at Oldham, and they had certainly come a long way after more than a decade of striving for success on a shoestring. Alex Ferguson – the picture of a disappointed man as he walked off the Wembley pitch – paid Joe Royle a handsome tribute as he left centre stage to Everton's team boss, while not forgetting, typically, to reflect upon his own team's misfortunes (skipper Steve Bruce, victim of a hamstring injury which had kept him out of the second-half action, revealed later that he had been playing in pain for weeks and would be undergoing a hernia operation).

United, it had to be admitted, had missed the magic of Eric Cantona and the wing wizardry of Andrei Kanchelskis; but Joe Royle maintained that his side had earned their victory – and who, on the day, could deny this? Sir Bobby Charlton was sporting enough to offer Royle a congratulatory handshake at the final whistle, and that was what you would have expected of him. Maybe, just there and then, Joe was prompted to reflect upon the might-have-beens. (Bobby Charlton, as a player, had been his idol, and they might even have become team-mates at Old Trafford.) Now, here was Joe, surveying the scene of his own managerial triumph.

It was in November 1994 that Royle had been asked to take on the job of steering beleaguered Everton to safety in the Premiership. He agreed to do it, even before he had settled the details of his contract at Goodison Park – that was how much Everton as a club still meant to him. Only a week before the 1955 FA Cup final, Royle had seen his efforts rewarded with success, as Everton squeezed a 1–0 victory out of Ipswich Town at Portman Road.

At Wembley, with their fans in full throttle as they roared their encouragement and their delight, Everton suddenly were not only safe and winners of the FA Cup, there was another bonus in store for them, because they were also in Europe. And with qualification for the Cup-Winners Cup there was the prospect of rich pickings on the Continent, not to mention lucrative deals from sponsorship. It was recorded that 'Everton have found a £10 million pot of gold at the end of the rainbow, while losers United have been told they cannot buy for the next three years unless current stars are sold first'.

So the fortunes of the Goodison club had altered dramatically in less than a couple of weeks. And one man who, it seemed, was seeking to share in the Goodison bonanza was Joe Royle's predecessor, Mike Walker. He had a Cup bonus written into his contract and, it was reported, this would have been worth £150,000 to him. But Everton were having none of this – director Cliff Finch spelled out the stand the club was making as he said: 'This suggestion is ludicrous. We had not even started the Cup campaign when he left.' Walker was still awaiting settlement of his contract, and Finch said: 'We are happy to negotiate a reasonable settlement – you have to make sure it is a one-off, final payment. In the next few days the two sides will be agreeing on a figure, and it will not include £150,000 for winning the FA Cup.' It seems logical and reasonable, however, to assume that Joe Royle could have expected to collect that Cup bonus, or something like it, as the manager who had taken them to victory at Wembley – plus, no doubt, a handsome reward for having ensured Premiership survival.

When Everton returned to Merseyside with the glittering trophy they had carried off at Wembley, there was a vociferous welcome from a crowd estimated to be 300,000 strong – and many of them were supporters of Liverpool.

Those fans of the Anfield Reds had seen their own team lift the Coca-Cola Cup and thus qualify for Europe; they had then savoured the delight of seeing their former idol, Kenny Dalglish, steering his Blackburn Rovers side to the Championship; and now here were Everton, conquerors of the old enemy, Manchester United, giving Merseyside another advantage as they cocked a snook at Manchester.

One man who was not deceived by all the euphoria, however – even though he enjoyed his moment of success to the full – was Everton's team boss. Joe Royle realised, better than anyone, just what was expected of him next. In a way, it was even more than the miracles he had been constantly performing during his time at Oldham. Everton, for the second season in succession, had managed to survive a battle to stay in the top flight; they were also in Europe. Now Royle was expected to build upon that and thrust the Goodison Park club into competition, on level terms, with Manchester United, Liverpool, Blackburn Rovers, Newcastle United, Leeds United, Arsenal – and any others who might bid for the game's major honours. Success, both at home and abroad, had become the target.

Whether Royle succeeds or fails in the quest to bring further trophies to Goodison remains to be seen; but I suspect that, win or lose, he may well come to the conclusion that Everton are to be his last club in football management. He had landed the job he dearly wanted, and he had been prepared to take the managerial risks involved – but it would not have escaped his attention that another former Goodison hero, Howard Kendall, had come so close to disaster the first time round, nor that he had bowed out after a somewhat torrid experience the second time. Kendall had even been a target for abuse, at one stage of his managerial career with Everton.

From the 1960s onwards, I covered the affairs of Everton FC and got to know many of its managers, players and officials well. I incurred the displeasure of Harry Catterick, watched with some sadness as Howard Kendall came under pressure from fans; and when it came to chairmen, one (George Watts) spoke of 'clobbering' me, had I been face to face with him, while another (John Moores) asked me how much I thought Everton should give Catterick as a bonus for winning the League. I also travelled abroad with Everton, to places like Milan and Zaragoza.

One day I saw Everton draw nil-nil against Wolves at Goodison Park, and afterwards all the reporters were agreed that while there had been no goals, this had been an absorbing and entertaining match. We were all astonished when Everton's manager of the day, the lean and hungry-looking Gordon Lee, came out to talk about his disappointment in the football – a 'hurry-scurry' game, Gordon called it. I saw Billy Bingham installed as Everton's team boss and I recall vividly the day Joe Royle made his Everton debut as a 16-year-old stripling. How can you forget, when the story you're covering turns out to be mostly about the irate fans assaulting and abusing the manager?

I saw a great deal of Joe Royle during his days as the manager of Oldham Athletic, too, and he went from Boundary Park, at long last, back to Goodison Park – no doubt, also, he was rewarded by a handsome rise in his pay packet. I can say, however, that while there are quite a few managers who are motivated at least as much by money as by the prospect of glory, Joe Royle is not one of them. As with Howard Kendall, managing Everton for him is an affair of the heart. While it was a wrench for him to leave Oldham after a dozen years on the roller-coaster there, the pull of Everton was too great. His first few months in charge of team affairs at Goodison Park saw him ending them in a blaze of glory. After which, as he well knew, he faced up to the sternest task of his managerial career – a career in which, unlike many others who have been on the treadmill, he has never so far been sacked. History will record how he handles the challenge.

Chapter Two

THE SWINGING SIXTIES

They were called (and still are called) the Swinging Sixties. It was an era when almost anything seemed to be permissible, and when it came to football, just about everything was happening. At club level, Everton carried off the Championship of the Football League, and then the FA Cup; at international level, England swept to success in the World Cup final; and in a much more modest way a young giant by the name of Joe Royle was taking his first steps along the road which would see him achieve fame twice over with the Goodison Park outfit which became known to the Everton faithful as the School of Soccer Science.

Three men could claim the credit for such a happy state of affairs during the 1960s. The first was an amiable Irishman by the name of Johnny Carey, who as a cultured defender had been a hero to the Old Trafford fans when he played for Manchester United. In fact, he was known to those fans as 'Gentleman Johnny'. The second was a man cast in somewhat different mould, because he gave the impression of being a dour character. His name was Harry Catterick, and he had played at centre-forward for Everton (though mostly in the reserve side). And the third individual was a bland-visaged but determined chap by the name of John Moores. He had made his fortune from the football pools – providing the coupons for the punters to fill in, rather than filling them in hopefully himself.

Johnny Carey had been introduced to the perils of management by Blackburn Rovers, who were later to employ two other future managers of Everton, Howard Kendall and Gordon Lee. Genial, pipe-smoking and a real gentleman, the bald-headed Carey claimed that the cause of his retirement as a player was a referee. 'I was going flat out one day, when I was passed by the referee,' was how he put it. He took charge of Blackburn Rovers and instilled into the side the art of playing cultured football in the Manchester United manner. Even so, promotion was not achieved during any of his first four seasons at Ewood Park – the Rovers finished third (a point adrift of the runners-up), sixth, fourth, and fourth again. Each time out, promotion slipped from their grasp in the final weeks of the campaign, yet the fans flocked to see the Rovers, who were nothing if not entertaining, not least when it came to scoring goals. By the mid-1950s, Carey had introduced a whippet-like Welsh youngster into the team – indeed, he became a member of the senior side while still eligible for the youth team. His name was Roy Vernon, and he was to become a major star with Everton. Another ace in the pack was Ronnie Clayton, who captained England, while Bryan Douglas and Ally MacLeod (yes, the one who became Scotland's team manager) were also first-team regulars.

Carey did indeed steer the Rovers to promotion, with a thrilling, last-gasp, 4–3 victory over their great challengers, Charlton Athletic, at The Valley. Charlton required only a draw; the Rovers had to win – and they did, in front of 70,000 partisan spectators. Not surprisingly, other clubs began to cast their eyes Carey's way, among them Everton, and though Blackburn said they would match what the Goodison Park club was prepared to pay, the attraction of greater resources proved too strong. So Blackburn Rovers lost their manager, and shortly afterwards they were to lose

Roy Vernon, whose career at Ewood Park seemed to take a downward turn. The Rovers had appointed Dally Duncan in succession to Carey, and Vernon appeared to have some problems in establishing a genuine rapport with his new boss. It wasn't long before Johnny Carey was back at Ewood Park, though only for a brief visit. He signed Vernon and let the Rovers have Eddie Thomas, a forward, plus £35,000. And so it was back to Everton, there to demonstrate that once again he could produce a team which played flowing football. This suited the fans but, unfortunately for Carey, chairman John Moores didn't appear to consider progress was being made swiftly enough. One afternoon, as the League clubs gathered in London for their annual meeting, the axe fell.

Carey and his chairman embarked upon a taxi ride together as they made their way towards the assembly of clubs; by the time they had stepped out of the vehicle, Carey had been informed that he was no longer the manager of Everton. He had been sacked – and in his place Moores installed Harry Catterick, who had come to his attention as the manager of Sheffield Wednesday. I had known Catterick during his days as the manager of Rochdale – I didn't own a car then, and I used to catch the bus from Manchester to Rochdale's Spotland ground, up on the hills. As I got to know Harry, we started to trust each other – he was suspicious generally of pressmen – and I used to take him out to lunch. We went in his car – a Ford Popular, as I recall – and the lunch cost around 3s 6d apiece. My treat.

Catterick had joined Everton as a player in 1937, and he was named as Rochdale's manager in 1951. By 1955 he had become the manager of Sheffield Wednesday, and he steered the acknowledged yo-yo team to promotion. In 1961, he succeeded Johnny Carey in the hot seat at Goodison Park, and he achieved what John Moores so fervently desired – he took Everton to Wembley twice, and to the pinnacle of the Football League, also on two occasions. Along the way, he – and Joe Royle – felt the backlash of the Everton fans' fury.

Along the way, too, I incurred the displeasure not only of Harry Catterick, but of John Moores.

Everton's chairman was what people used to call a self-made man. He had invested £50 in a business venture with two other men, but when it seemed as if the venture – football pools – was about to sink without trace, Moores bought his partners out, convinced his family to join him in working round the clock, and the result was that Littlewoods Pools eventually became the biggest in the world. By the time he was 35, John Moores had become a millionaire. I got to know him well – indeed, I believe I became closer to him than any other journalist of the time. Somewhat cheekily, I not only found out his office number, but I rang him, and to my surprise, I managed to engineer an appointment to see him. We got on well, and I became a regular visitor to his panelled office in Cases Street, Liverpool, where his secretary, Miss Mitchell, would appear with the tea service. John Moores came to trust me, and I began to get some good stories from him about Everton's plans as they concerned players on the books and players in the pipeline.

There was only one fly in the ointment; Harry Catterick didn't approve of the goings-on. He wanted Everton's business to remain confidential all the time (and who could blame him?). He didn't want stories about ventures into the transfer market splashed across the back page of *The People* newspaper, which employed me. He had a difficult enough job as it was – indeed, there was a time when, driving home after a match, he took himself off to hospital because he was suffering chest pains, and there was speculation as to whether or not this meant a heart attack. Happily, he recovered and carried on being a football manager.

Harry realised early on during his career that it was not enough just to be a manager involved with players; so he learned to read balance sheets and thus gained an insight into what makes a football club tick – and what makes a man like John Moores a millionaire. Harry was also a stickler for discipline. He had been largely responsible for the inception of the magnificent Bellefield training ground, and his players had to book in there – the apprentices at nine o'clock in a morning and the senior professionals one hour later. Once the signing-in books had been removed, if your name was missing you had to come up with a very good explanation for it. And certainly Everton's players were not encouraged to talk to the press.

So Harry Catterick ran a very tight ship, and he ruled almost with a rod of iron, aided and abetted by a trainer called Wilf Dixon, who often looked stern and unbending. There was also a long-serving chief scout called Harry Cooke, and so Everton had a triumvirate which kept a close eye on just about every department on the playing side. With John Moores at the helm, and the Championship the major target, there was money to spend on reinforcements, and it wasn't long before Harry Catterick had added to the talent inherited from Johnny Carey's day.

You could look around and see footballers with an international pedigree a yard long; and while Catterick knew all about the need to balance the books, he was able to go out and splash record fees upon big names in his efforts to make Everton Football Club the finest in the League. He succeeded in no small way, as he attracted star players while, at the same time, not neglecting to groom local talent. In this manner he achieved a blend which measured up to the requirements of skill and strength, and he satisfied the desire of John Moores to make Everton the team all the others had to beat.

I got to know nearly all the big-name players at Goodison Park: Gordon West in goal, Alan Ball, Alex Parker at full-back, Brian Labone at centre-half, Joe Royle at centre-forward, Alex Young, Roy Vernon and Billy Bingham, a winger who became Everton's manager himself in later days. Indeed, Billy and I had a row one day after I had run a story suggesting that he was ready to shake the dust of Goodison

Park from his feet – he accused me of having got him into trouble with his manager. I stood up for myself, because I knew I had right on my side, and I'm happy to say that we soon became friends again.

Gordon West cost Everton around £27,000 when he was signed from Blackpool, a fee which exceeded the world-record £23,000 Manchester United had paid Doncaster Rovers for Harry Gregg. Catterick, then the manager of Sheffield Wednesday, had been tipped to land Gregg, but it was Harry Catterick himself who told me: 'Forget about him joining us – he's going to Manchester United.' And so it proved. I rang Matt Busby at his home on the Saturday evening, managed to get him to confirm that he had put in an offer for Gregg, and had an exclusive, back-page lead on the deal. Later, Catterick sold one of his Wednesday players – the so-called golden boy Albert Quixall – to Manchester United for what then was considered an astonishing amount of money: £45,000.

West, who turned down the chance to go to the World Cup with Alf Ramsey in 1970, was an amiable giant of a man, while Alan Ball was built on much less of a frame, yet Bally never shirked a tackle in his life. He told me how he had promised his dad that if he let him become a footballer, he would play for England by the time he was 20. He achieved this objective by playing for England in the World Cup final triumph of 1966. He also turned on a display against Everton, before that, which Joe Royle will never forget; because it led to the Everton supporters giving Harry Catterick a hard time of it, to say the least. Catterick had dropped the 'Golden Vision', Alex Young, in favour of the 16-year-old Royle. That was for a match against Blackpool at Bloomfield Road. Everton lost to a Blackpool side inspired by Ball, and afterwards furious Everton fans turned on Catterick, pinning him against the team coach as they railed him for having ditched Young.

It wasn't long before Catterick was going back to

Bloomfield Road – to spend £110,000 of Everton's money on Alan Ball; and there was quite a drama about the signing, too, because Leeds United and Stoke City became rivals for the player's signature. Young Ball's father (also named Alan) was coaching Stoke – I had played a part in getting him the job there – but when it all came down to it, Leeds and Everton were the clubs which mattered. At the time, Bally had claimed a World Cup-winners' medal and, of course, there had been a great deal of speculation as to whether or not Blackpool could hang on to him.

Don Revie's Leeds had stated publicly that they had made their offer, and they wouldn't go any higher, while Harry Catterick had indicated that though he thought Ball was a fair player, Everton had no intention of paying an outrageous fee for him. In fact, Everton's chairman at the time, Holland Hughes, had merely said, with a bland expression on his face, that 'Everton are always interested in good players'. As for Blackpool, they were ready to offer Ball a four-year deal at £100 a week and chuck in £10,000 as a signing-on bonus, but it was after a pre-season match against Preston that the die was cast. Young Ball, who had been the star of the match, made up his mind to resist all Blackpool's overtures.

He told me all about it himself – how, the following Monday, it really became make-up-your-mind time, as Everton swooped, with Leeds even then striving to win the battle. That was the day that Blackpool were due to meet Preston in the return game at Bloomfield Road and, as usual, Bally travelled from his home on the outskirts of Bolton. He was relaxing in a café, having a cup of coffee after having done a spot of light training, when team-mate Hughie Fisher appeared, looking, according to Ball, 'as if he'd run a mile in three minutes flat'. He told Ball: 'The boss wants to see you, right away.'

When Ball returned to Bloomfield Road, he was greeted with the news that manager Ronnie Suart was in his office – along with Harry Catterick. And for a few seconds young Ball found himself wishing it had been Matt Busby of Manchester United, which was his favourite club outside the one for which he played. But, on Monday, 15 August – just five days before the big kick-off – the deal was set in motion. Catterick wasted no time in persuading Alan Ball to join his star-studded squad, pointing out that he must sign by six o'clock that evening to become eligible to play for Everton in the European Cup-winners Cup competition, so a swift decision had to be made. Ball asked for time to talk to his father at Stoke, and after a brief chat he told Catterick he would join the Goodison club. He was to figure in one of football's most famous partnerships – with Howard Kendall and Colin Harvey – and enjoy further success, this time at club level.

It all seemed a far cry from the days when he had been at odds with his home-town club, Bolton Wanderers, and getting into the kind of trouble on the field which had him tagged as a player whose fiery temper matched his red hair. Indeed, on one occasion, Ball senior had been told: 'Your son will never make anything, except a jockey.' And when young Ball's all-or-nothing style of play was called into question, the remark was passed that 'it would do your lad good to get his ankle broken – he holds the ball too much'. So, after such acrimony, young Ball obtained his release from Bolton and caught a bus to sign for Blackpool.

Bolton must have pondered on what might have been, when they learned that Alan Ball had joined Everton for a record-breaking fee of £110,000; and Leeds manager Don Revie was left to sigh with regret, too. Unknown to Ball, Revie – having learned that Harry Catterick was Blackpool-bound – had got on the phone to Ronnie Suart and was making it clear he wanted to be in at the death. Suart by that time had agreed terms with Everton, so he was in a spot. Revie, it was said, even set out by car, ready to make a dash to Blackpool in a bid to beat Everton to the punch. Whether or not he heard the news of the transfer on his car radio no one knew, but he never appeared at Bloomfield Road, and so

Ball became an Everton player. Thus he joined a list of personalities who were already household names in the world of football.

Like Alan Ball, Howard Kendall and Colin Harvey, Joe Royle was to figure in Everton's second Championship success under the management of Harry Catterick. And it hadn't taken Catterick long to do the business after his arrival from Hillsborough, where he had taken Sheffield Wednesday to the very brink of the Championship (they finished as runners-up to Spurs at the end of season 1960–61). It was then that Catterick became labelled 'Mr Success', after a popular song of the time. The sacking of Johnny Carey was followed, on 17 April 1961, by the shock news that Catterick was returning to Goodison Park, where he was remembered as a smallish centre-forward from the post-war years. He had joined Everton as a part-time professional at the age of 17.

Catterick's first match in charge of team affairs at Everton was against none other than Sheffield Wednesday, at Hillsborough; and, naturally, there was a certain amount of tension in the air as the teams went out to do battle. Everton won the duel by the odd goal in three, and by the end of the season they were finishing in fifth place. By the time Catterick had completed his first full term as their manager, Everton had improved to finish fourth and then, at the end of season 1962–63, they captured the League title. The ambitions of chairman John Moores had been satisfied – for the time being, at any rate.

Johnny Carey may well have felt that he deserved some of the credit for the title success, because he had been instrumental in taking some of the big-name players to Goodison Park and embarking upon the flowing football which earned the team such a good name among the fans, but it was Catterick who honed the side into a Championship-winning outfit, as he added a touch of steel to Everton's footballing make-up. This fellow, born in

Darlington and a junior with Stockport County when he first came to Everton's attention, was a stickler for detail, and he had had a good grounding. After playing as the deputy to the great Tommy Lawton, he had embarked upon a new career as player-manager at Crewe, then gone to Rochdale and on to Sheffield Wednesday. When it came to the financial side of football, he was shrewd as well. 'I heard about one manager who joined a small club and he immediately raised the wages to such a level they would have had to fill the ground every week to meet the bill. A manager must be aware of the financial situation and understand the administration.' He certainly did.

So did John Moores. I was in his office one afternoon after Everton had claimed the title trophy when he threw the question at me: 'How much do you think we should give Harry, as a bonus for winning the Championship?' It took me by surprise, but – thinking as quickly as possible – I answered back: 'Well, I should think £1,000 . . .' That, of course, was no small amount of money at the start of the 1960s. But, just in case I'd done Harry a disservice, I quickly added: 'Tax free, of course.' I never learned if Harry did get £1,000 as a bonus; nor did I ever discover if he knew John Moores had sought my advice. Moores himself was not a flashy sort of man – I found him down-to-earth and easy to talk to. On another occasion when I was in his office, he answered the phone and it became apparent that his daughter was calling. I saw him start to smile and, as it became clear that she was announcing her intention to visit, I heard him say: 'Oh, your Mam will be pleased to see you.'

Neither John Moores nor Harry Catterick was pleased with me, however, on other occasions and, finally, Moores cut me off without a penny, as the saying goes. There came a day when Catterick, fed up with seeing stories about Everton splashed across the back page of my paper, *The People*, complained to his chairman, who rang me up to tell me about it, and summoned me to a meeting with himself and his manager. I told Moores I didn't think it would do any good, but I went anyway and we discussed our mutual problems. I wanted stories, Harry wanted to keep club business to himself. Naturally, we had to agree to differ, although I continued to visit John Moores and tried to be as circumspect as possible, without losing out.

As a result of having won the League Championship, Everton went into the European Champions Cup competition, and they were pitched against Inter Milan, managed by the legendary Helenio Herrera. This was the man who, it was said, had taught the football world just how to turn the 'beautiful game' (Pelé's description) into one of great defensive skill. Helenio Herrera's parents came from Andalusia, a region in southern Spain, but they moved to Argentina, and he was born there. The family finally retraced its steps to Europe, and Herrera's career in football was studded with trophies as he managed Barcelona (the title twice, the old European Fairs Cup twice, in the space of three years) and Inter Milan (three League Championships, two European Cup triumphs). Herrera became the acknowledged maestro, while in the early 1960s Harry Catterick was the European novice, as Everton tried conclusions with Inter. Indeed, it could be said that there was no manager more famous than Helenio throughout the world; he was once asked where he thought he would finish, if a popularity poll of personalities were to be held in Italy. His recorded reply: 'Behind Sophia Loren – but only because she has a better figure.'

Herrera, who was lionised, made the claim that he was the first player to have taken up the role of sweeper. That was when he was pursuing his career in France. His team was leading by the only goal, with around quarter of an hour to go, and it was then, he claimed, that he ordered a team-mate to take his place while he dropped back behind the defence. His side won, and Herrera never forgot the role he had played, once he graduated to management. According to

Herrera, many people criticised *catenaccio* because it was a system which was misused: 'Managers who imitated me did not let their backs attack; they used *catenaccio* as a defensive system.' Herrera reckoned that Italian ace Giacinto Fachetti, who captained his country on 70 occasions, was able to join in attacking moves at Inter 'because of me'.

Supremely successful at club level, Herrera also managed international sides in Spain, France and Italy. Just in case it might appear as if Senor Herrera never made a mistake, however, there was one occasion during his reign in Spain when he found himself under the cosh. It happened after his team, Barcelona, had lost to arch-rivals Real Madrid and he was assaulted by fans outside the team's hotel. Herrera travelled widely; he learned much (he became proficient in Arabic, French and Italian, as well as Spanish); and even coming up to the mid-1990s he was still in gainful employment.

At that stage of his life, he had turned 70 and was enjoying himself as a television commentator. But he had his memories of soccer battles won and lost and, in his days as manager of Barcelona, he had seen his side defeat Wolves 5–2 at Molineux where the home side rarely lost. That was in 1960, and afterwards he was moved to observe to journalists that 'you in England are playing now in the style we Continentals used so many years ago, with much physical strength, but no method, no technique'. He claimed that when it came to modern football, 'the Britons missed the evolution. That was the case when we played Wolves.' He went on to explain that we had missed the evolution because 'the English are creatures of habit'.

When he left Barcelona for Inter Milan, there was no difference in mentality between the two teams, because the Latins were so much alike. And under the guidance of Helenio Herrera, Inter flourished. Not for nothing did the Italian fans refer to him as Il Mago – The Magician. And he was still listened to with respect as he offered his views on Silvio Berlusconi's Canale 5 television programme in the early 1990s. This, then, was the man whom Harry Catterick, manager of the English League champions, had to contend with in the very first round of the European Champions Cup, after that title success of season 1962–63.

Naturally, there was tremendous interest in the Everton-Inter clash, especially with the return having to be played in Milan, after the first leg had ended in stalemate. I was one of the pressmen who travelled with Harry Catterick and his team, and the omens were hardly propitious from the outset, as we gathered at Manchester airport for the trip. We were informed that our flight would be delayed, because there were storms over the Alps and our aircraft would not be able to get above them.

So off we went to the restaurant, to enjoy a free dinner and ponder upon what time we would finally take off that evening. Eventually, we discovered that we would no longer be flying directly to Milan. Instead, we would have to take a plane to London, where we would board a Comet and continue our journey long through the night. It wasn't what you could call a flying start.

I sat up front alongside the *Daily Mirror*'s Frank McGhee, and we enjoyed the hospitality offered. Frank fell asleep before long, and didn't waken up until we were just about to land; my stomach had reacted in a different manner, and I hadn't slept a wink. We landed in the early hours and eventually reached our hotel, at Monza, where the staff prepared coffee and sandwiches for us before we all trooped off to bed. As I sat with two or three of the Everton players, chatting about nothing in particular while we drank our coffee on the terrace, John Moores came over. 'I hope you're not going to do anything naughty, Mr Liversedge,' he said, his eyes twinkling – and as I smiled back, I wondered for a moment if he had decided to have his little joke, or if he had been prompted by a suspicious manager to have a quiet word with me.

Everton threw the young Colin Harvey in for the match against Inter, played in front of 80,000 people in the famous San Siro stadium. It was quite a night for Everton and Harvey to make their bow away in European football – the Italians had already done the hard bit at Goodison Park in August 1963 by holding Everton to a scoreless draw. Jimmy Gabriel missed the return through injury, Dennis Stevens switched to right-half, and Harvey – retiring and modest, and just 18 years old – found himself being given the berth at inside-right. He had thought he was going along for the ride but he found himself doing battle against Inter – and giving a good account of himself.

As I recall, Roy Vernon (the man who was, unwittingly, to cost me my friendly relationship with John Moores) played a lone hand up front, and I felt that night that if Catterick had been a touch more adventurous and thrown everything in against Inter, there might have been a turn-up for the book. As it was, Inter pressed forward time and again, urged on by their fanatical supporters; yet for long spells Everton managed to keep their opponents at bay – indeed, at one stage you sensed that the home fans were beginning to become as frustrated as their team, and that it wouldn't take much to make them turn on Herrera. He must have been feeling somewhat uncomfortable as the minutes ticked by but, eventually, the inevitable happened. Everton succumbed to the continuous pressure, and conceded the vital goal.

It was sufficient to win the match for the Italians, and so Everton went out of the European Cup, first pop (in 1966, they were to go out of the Cup-Winners Cup, beaten by Real Zaragoza). The players were very disappointed at the result. Back at the hotel, they disappeared one by one, presumably to their beds or to go out for a few beers.

As the *Sunday Mirror*'s Edgar Turner and I sat having a drink, with the night getting late, we realised there was a bit of a commotion going on, and we discovered that the staff were getting irate because two of the Everton players, feeling hungry, had gone in search of food and raided the kitchen. There was talk of getting Signor Catterick out of bed and making a big thing of it, but Edgar and I managed to calm down the duty manager, and we plied him with enough drinks until he had mellowed sufficiently to feel that honour had been satisfied. No more was said, and Signor Catterick never got to know about this minor international incident; neither did chairman Moores.

One of the players on Everton's books at the start of the 1960s was a chunky little inside-forward who had been recruited from Celtic. His name was Bobby Collins, and this Scotland international, while not quite as barrel-chested as Dave Mackay, was just as influential on the field of play and feared no opponent. Bobby and I struck up a friendship which has lasted to this day, and I played a small (and, as it turned out, meaningless) part in his £25,000 transfer to Leeds United. It began when Bobby rang to break the shock news that Harry Catterick was prepared to sell him, and that struggling Leeds United had agreed terms for his transfer. Bobby wanted some advice before setting off across the Pennines to meet Don Revie the following day, so I told him: 'You can stay at my house tonight, and we'll have a good talk about all the ins and outs of it.' When he arrived, we went through every aspect of the proposed deal.

The following morning, as I prepared to go to work, Bobby – who didn't really want to leave Everton and appeared reluctant to join such a struggling outfit as Leeds – prepared to drive over to meet Revie. My final words to him, more or less, were these: 'Whatever you do, don't sign on the dotted line today, even though Revie will try to persuade you to sign before the five o'clock deadline [which would make Bobby eligible to play for Leeds on the Saturday]. Remember, once the word gets out that you're up for sale, who knows which clubs will come in for you? You could find you've got plenty of choice.' I felt that this was wise advice, and I pointed out that Leeds themselves, if they wanted him so much, would almost certainly remain in the hunt, even if the deadline came and went. 'They'll still want you next week, and if nobody does come in, then you can still sign for Don Revie.' Bobby concurred with this sage advice, and set off for Elland Road.

I had also told him to let me know how things had gone, once he had talked to Revie (whom I knew could be persuasive) and, sure enough, I received a phone call later in the day. I must admit that Bobby Collins sounded somewhat sheepish as he informed me: 'I've signed for Leeds.' And he didn't say a word as I told him: 'You bloody fool!' At any rate, the deed had been done, and that was that. We didn't fall out, of course, and I wished Bobby all the best. As events turned out, my advice had not been all that good, and Bobby's decision to throw in his lot with Leeds was proved to have been extremely sensible. He became their midfield general, inspiring a revival which took Leeds to the final of the FA Cup, into Europe and other honours. He even made a comeback after having broken a leg while playing against Continental opposition. In short, his transfer to Leeds United made him a hero all over again, and turned out to have been the best possible move he could have made. So much for well-meant advice.

Harry Catterick, not for the first time, had elected to sell a player who had been a hero to the fans, and Everton still managed to press on to further success, in the shape of the FA Cup, a second appearance at Wembley, and another League Championship. Even so, there were a few scares for manager and fans along the way – indeed, Catterick's career seemed to be at the crossroads midway through the afternoon of the 1966 FA Cup final.

Chapter Three

A WINNING GAMBLE

The FA Cup final of 1966 might well have spelled the beginning of the end for Harry Catterick as manager of Everton, because he took a gamble which, to say the least, looked very much as if it had backfired upon him and upon his club. The occasion was laced with spice because, when Everton arrived at their final destination, they were coming up against Catterick's old club, Sheffield Wednesday, at Wembley. Wednesday had some good players of their own, not least Peter Eustace, Ron Springett and Jim McCalliog, while they had an up-and-coming centre-half by the name of Sam Ellis. He was just 19 years old when Wednesday pitched him into the Cup-final fray.

As for Catterick, he took a massive gamble, too, because he had to make a straight choice between his £80,000 marksman, Fred Pickering, and the virtually unrated Mike Trebilcock, a young Cornishman whom Everton had snapped up from Plymouth Argyle for what really amounted to peanuts. Pickering had kicked off with Blackburn Rovers as a full-back, but he had hardly made his mark in that position; however, when he was switched to lead the Rovers attack, he swiftly showed that he knew how to beat defenders and find the net. He became a prolific marksman – which, of course, was why Harry Catterick was prepared to speculate £80,000 of his club's cash to land him.

Unfortunately for Everton, Pick sustained an injury which didn't do his chances of playing at Wembley much good but, ultimately, he declared himself fit enough to take the chance, and so the final decision had to come from Catterick.

When the Cup-ties first came along, keeper Gordon West was just about fit again after having sustained an injury, but during his absence Geoff Barnett (later transferred to Arsenal) had been given his chance and done well. However, Everton's last League game before the Cup was at Blackpool, and they had lost 2–0. So West regained his place and, as he told me later, but for that defeat 'I might never have had the chance to play at Wembley'. So West was in, and when Harry Catterick made his decision about the front-line job, Fred Pickering was out. Gordon West told me: 'I could see tears in Fred's eyes when he realised he was going to be a spectator on the big occasion.'

Wednesday set about Everton to some tune – they had gone two goals up almost before the Everton players realised what had hit them. Those goals from McCalliog and Ford had set Wednesday alight, and Everton were really struggling to make an impact – so much so that their fans were not only starting to become restive, they were beginning to make their feelings known in a very vocal manner. The cry went up: 'Pickering! Pickering!' But Fred Pickering was powerless to intervene. As for Catterick, he had to sit there and sweat it out, along with the strident fans, knowing that he was most certainly not in their good books at that point.

Wednesday were still dictating the way the game went; Everton seemed unable to get into their sweet-flowing stride. And, as Gordon West confessed to me later, he felt he would be taking the blame for having allowed the ball to go past him for Wednesday's second goal. But, at long last, the prayers of the Everton faithful were answered, and deliverance came for both West and Catterick. Mike Trebilcock, the makeweight striker who had not found favour with the fans, gave his side new hope as he beat keeper Ron Springett to narrow the gap to 2–1. And, as Wednesday were still striving to regain their composure after this setback, Everton, with their tails well and truly up, struck again. Once more, it was Trebilcock who did the damage; and after that there was no holding Harry Catterick's team. They tore into their opponents.

Still the clock ticked on, however, and it began to look as if the best Everton would manage was to take Wednesday into extra time. But the football fates still had one more card to deal, and it fell Everton's way. Left-winger Derek Temple was the man who broke the deadlock and saw Sheffield Wednesday off, as Everton surged forward and Temple delivered the knock-out blow. The scene was almost indescribable – Wembley was in uproar, and one Everton fan raced on to the pitch to convey his delight to the players. The police gave chase, the fan fled, twisting this way and that – and, when he was finally halted, he wriggled out of his jacket and was on the move again. At last, he was brought to earth and everyone was able to settle back. The final whistle was blown and the 1966 FA Cup final was all over. Result: Everton 3, Sheffield Wednesday 2.

Hurriedly, Gordon West picked up not only his cap, but the front false tooth which he had deposited in the cap before the action began. Back in the Everton dressing-room lay a good-luck charm which left-back Ramon Wilson had given Gordon when the Cup run had begun. The charm was in the shape of a little ginger-haired man, and West had taken 'Ginger', as he called him, along to every Cup match in which Everton had played. Halfway through the Wembley final, however, it had seemed that Ginger would no longer be bringing Everton good fortune. Now, West and his delighted team-mates were walking up the steps to the royal box to be presented with their winners medals by Princess Margaret, while Sheffield Wednesday's players were still striving to come to terms with the dramatic manner in which they had let slip their two-goal advantage. And, of course, Harry Catterick's choice of Mike Trebilcock had been well and truly vindicated. Manager and player were heroes to the fans – which showed just how fortunes can change in the space of mere minutes, never mind an hour and a half.

Footballers tend to be superstitious – Don Revie had a 'lucky' blue jacket, for example, and at Everton there were quite a few players who looked to Lady Luck, as well as to their own footballing ability. Colin Harvey, for instance, used to sit in the dressing-room with his head held between his hands. Gordon West told me: 'Sometimes, I would swear he was praying.'

Alan Ball always used to be the first to get in line for the pre-match 'chest rub', while West himself refused to fasten the laces of his boots until centre-half Brian Labone had fastened his. As captain, 'Labby' was first out on to the pitch; then came the keeper, followed by right-back Tommy Wright. John Hurst, once he had changed into his playing kit, always wore his wrist watch over the sleeve of his jersey, not far from his elbow.

It is worth pointing out that Harry Catterick, with his mind ever on the need to balance the books, groomed home-grown talent as well as splashing out with the cheque book. Come to that, he recouped the cash Everton had paid for Bobby Collins when he joined them from Celtic, while the transfer of Alan Ball to Arsenal brought Everton a £5,000 profit on the £110,000 they had handed over to Blackpool.

The home-produced talent? There was Tommy Wright, Brian Labone, Brian Harris, Colin Harvey, Derek Temple, Alan Whittle and, of course, Joe Royle. Joe didn't figure in the 1966 FA Cup-final side, but his time was shortly to come. And there was more, much more than the FA Cup in the air at Goodison Park during the heady days of 1966. By the summer, England – Alan Ball included – were on their way to triumph at Wembley in the final of the World Cup, while at Goodison Park and Old Trafford some of the pre-final matches were staged. I covered World Cup games at both these grounds, and I was privileged to see some of the world's finest footballers in action.

Joe Royle's Everton career had been launched, in a fashion, with a telephone call which prompted him to pay a visit to Liverpool's famous Penny Lane, the one which was set to music by the Beatles. The man who made the phone call was a headmaster by the name of Dave McKay, whose school, Ranworth Square County Primary, was attended by Joe Royle. McKay had called to say that Joe should present himself at Penny Lane for a game of football – one which, it transpired, was being watched by the fellows whose job it was to pick the Liverpool Schoolboy team. It was a Saturday afternoon in 1961, and it turned out to be an important day in Joe's young life.

The Schoolboy selectors were sufficiently impressed to choose him for their junior side and, of course, the 12-year-old, football-daft lad jumped at the chance. Three years later, he was asked to put pen to paper and join Harry Catterick's Everton. Neither Joe Royle nor Everton was to regret this.

Joe had played in his first competitive football match at the tender age of seven – for Ranworth Square's 'B' team against Warbreck Road County Primary – and the game was played on a cinder pitch, with young Royle wearing a pair of big old-fashioned boots. He was at inside-right, he scored a goal, and his team won 3–0. Little did he dream then that at the ripe old age of 19 he would be walking out at Wembley to play for Everton in the final of the FA Cup. But it wasn't roses, roses all the way, because first he had to make a complete recovery from a broken leg (that took all of three months) and then he had to bounce back after having made his Everton debut at 16 and being sent back to the reserves.

As a kid, Joe Royle idolised Manchester United, and although he lived no more than a stone's throw from Anfield, he dreamed of stepping out on the pitch at Old Trafford as one of Matt Busby's famous Babes. In fact, he was to talk to both Busby and Liverpool manager Bill Shankly before joining Everton, which spoke volumes for the potential talent the big three clubs had spotted in this raw-boned youngster. It was when the young Royle left Ranworth Square for Quarry Bank High School that he became a member of the Under-12 team. At that stage he had been playing at centre-half, with the odd appearance up front. And he still managed to end the season as his side's leading scorer.

Centre-half or centre-forward? That was the kind of problem Joe Royle found himself being called upon to decide in later years, only this time it wasn't his own career which was at stake. When he managed Oldham Athletic, he and a player he had signed from Everton were at odds over the player's best position.

One of the remarkable things about the way Royle's career has gone is the fact that Anfield has played a significant part, even though he turned down the chance to sign on for Bill Shankly. Not only did Joe play for Liverpool Boys, he was chosen to play for Lancashire Boys – and that was when he and Liverpool's current manager, Roy Evans, became team-mates. It was Royle, of Liverpool Boys, at right-half, Evans, of Bootle Boys, at left-half, when they teamed up together in the Lancashire Under-15 side in season 1963–64. They were together four times all told, and never once did they finish on the winning side. Evans went on to play for England Schoolboys, but while Joe Royle received an invitation to try his luck, he was unable to make the final trials.

Evans joined Liverpool, his one and only love, but became almost a permanent reserve. He figured in the first team fewer than a dozen times, and when he was offered a backroom job at the age of 26 he pondered long and hard, then decided to take it. He said, rightly, that it had been no disgrace not to make it at Liverpool as a regular first-teamer, considering the strength in depth and the amount of talent there was at Anfield. As the years rolled by, he saw Shankly succeeded by Bob Paisley, then it was Joe Fagan and Kenny Dalglish – and all the time Roy Evans waited in the wings, although his role on the backroom side increased in importance. Not until Graeme Souness had been and gone did he finally get the chance to be his own man, and after his early spell in charge he was rewarded with a contract to take him through to 1998.

Joe Royle, meanwhile, enjoyed success as a player, because he went on to wear the white jersey of England at full international level. As for Anfield and that connection with footballing fate, he was to say, on his return there as Everton's manager: 'It's strange how this ground keeps on recurring in my life.'

Although he had made his first-team debut for Everton at the tender age of 16, Joe had had to wait until he was 18 years old before he was given the opportunity to figure in a Merseyside derby game, and when he reflected upon matches in which he tangled with the likes of Iron Man Tommy Smith and Ron Yeats (the player Bill Shankly had introduced to the press as 'a Colossus'), he reckoned: 'That was different!' One of Joe's enduring memories of the 1969–70 Championship season was of derby games. 'After having lost 3–0 to Liverpool at Goodison Park, we went to Anfield and won the return 2–0 . . . and I was fortunate enough to score. Our Championship season would have been tainted, if Liverpool had managed to beat us twice.'

And while Joe Royle has enjoyed success since he became a manager, taking two different clubs to Wembley, he still rates playing as the greatest part of the game. As he put it: 'We're still frustrated players. As managers, we play the games through somebody else's legs. The thrills we have are now second-hand.' He wasn't the first manager, and he won't be the last, to utter such sentiments, either. As for his loyalty to Everton, that has never altered through the years – although the same cannot be said about two of the players who figured in Liverpool's line-up against the Blues during the mid-1990s, because both Ian Rush and Steve McManaman started out as Everton supporters. Indeed, in 1984, when Everton went to Wembley to meet and beat Watford in the final of the FA Cup, the tousle-haired young McManaman stood patiently in line, along with his dad, waiting to pick up his Wembley ticket. At that stage of his life, he dreamed of playing for Everton and his idols were Bob Latchford and Duncan McKenzie. When he did put pen to paper, however, it was to sign for Liverpool – and he went back to Wembley to earn an FA Cup-winners' medal against Sunderland, then became a two-goal hero as Liverpool won the 1995 Coca-Cola Cup final against Bolton Wanderers. Not many weeks later, Joe Royle was at Wembley, too – enjoying success against Manchester United and looking ahead to more derby thrillers against Liverpool . . . not least at the ground 'across the park' which held so many memories for him.

It was at Anfield that he made his debut as a Manchester City player, and after he had steered Oldham Athletic into the Premier League, their first-ever fixture in the top flight was against Liverpool, at Anfield. They lost that day, after having taken the lead through Earl Barrett (later to rejoin Royle at Goodison Park), but they survived in the top flight, and when they tried their luck there on another occasion, Liverpool manager Graeme Souness paid Joe Royle and his men this compliment: 'Oldham have had their problems since winning promotion at the end of the 1990–91 season but, to their credit, they have never disbanded belief in attacking and entertaining football. They can spring a surprise anywhere at any time; let's have no doubt about that. And Joe Royle has earned his respected reputation through consistently good work at Boundary Park.'

Oldham almost, but not quite, sprang a surprise that day at Anfield, but in the end they failed to stay in the Premiership, while Graeme Souness – whose Liverpool side was sunk in a relegation battle (for Oldham) at Boundary Park some time later – moved out and Roy Evans was given his chance. But all this was almost light years ahead, as the young Joe Royle pursued what he hoped would become a successful career in professional football. During season 1963–64, when he was going great guns with Liverpool Boys, they drew big crowds and got results. When Liverpool's youngsters met London Boys in a friendly match at Goodison Park one cold winter's night in 1963, no fewer than 10,000 folk turned up to watch the talent on parade.

One contemporary report said: 'Many managers of struggling professional clubs must have looked with envy at the size of the Goodison gate. More than 10,000 people turned out on a bitterly cold night to see Liverpool in action and provide still more evidence of a fanatical enthusiasm for the game in this city. The schoolboys who made up most of the crowd had not been slow to learn from their fathers. They greeted the sides with "When the Saints Go Marching In", and soon switched to chanting "Everton!", at regular intervals.' Liverpool boys repaid their fans' faith by collecting four trophies – the only one they failed to win was the English Schoolboys Trophy. Yet Joe Royle still wasn't the centre-forward he became – he played only a few games in attack, but contrived to end up as the team's leading scorer, with 15 goals to his credit.

According to Joe himself, he was happiest while playing in defence, especially when he was given a role at right-half. Later, he was to admit that while this position suited him down to the ground, Everton were to prove him wrong, as they converted him to the job of being a full-time centre-forward. Harry Catterick may not have been a star striker himself, but he certainly recognised the attacking potential of the young Joe Royle, and he got the best out of him. But before Joe became a professional at Goodison, he achieved a distinction other than that of a marksman: he was named captain of the Lancashire Boys team. Then came one of the greatest disappointments of his young life: while Roy Evans made it into the English Schoolboy side, Joe had to turn down the chance to play in the final trials because of his school football commitments.

That blow, and the broken leg, taught him a lesson which he never forgot: that it's no use moaning about your bad luck – you just have to get on with life. And it's a credo which he has believed in, right through his professional career. There may be those who would claim that Joe Royle, in fact, is too genial a character and that he should have been more ruthless both as a player and as a manager, but anyone who thinks he is a soft touch should think again. When necessary, he can play the tough guy.

It was when Everton's chief scout, Harry Cooke, called upon the Royle family that the prospect of a career in professional football really opened up for Joe. Cooke had seen the lad playing at right-half for Liverpool Boys against Wigan Boys – a match Liverpool won 3–0 – and had clearly been impressed. Not long after that, it became apparent that Everton were not the only club in the hunt, as both Liverpool and Manchester United declared their interest. Everton continued to monitor the youngster, with one of their scouts, Matt McPeake, a regular watcher. Harry Catterick also took the trouble to check on Joe when he played for Lancashire against Cheshire. Lancashire lost by the odd goal in three, but their goal was scored by young Royle. The lad hadn't been aware of Catterick's presence, but he learned from McPeake that Everton's manager had been duly impressed – sufficiently impressed to be considering offering Joe the chance to join the Goodison club.

But by that time Liverpool and United were also showing their hand, and when it came down to it, Joe Royle was being asked to talk not only to Everton, but to the Anfield and Old Trafford clubs. It was a dazzling prospect for a teenager – three of the top clubs in football, and each one wanting to sign him. Naturally, Joe Royle visited Anfield and Old Trafford – and maybe the odds at that stage were on him becoming a Busby Babe. He met Matt Busby, listened to what he had to say, and was duly impressed; then he talked to Bill Shankly, heard all about the advantages of signing for Liverpool, and was impressed all over again. Last of all came Harry Catterick and Everton, and then it was time to make the big decision.

For some reason which he could not quite define, Joe never really fancied going to Liverpool – it's something which has stuck with him, too, right through his career. He has seemed reluctant to go to Anfield, other than in the line of business; although, of course, he has nothing against the club and, indeed, has great admiration for what Liverpool have achieved through the years. As for Manchester United, they finished second-best when it came to making a choice – and this, despite the hero-worship of Joe Royle for Bobby Charlton. Everton it was, and so the decision was made. It has to be admitted that Joe's headmaster, Dave McKay, was an Everton fan, and he played a part in advising the youngster to take his chance with the Goodison club. It turned out to be sound advice, and Joe Royle went on to make his mark.

Not that he struck gold at the start – indeed, he got a bit of an eye-opener when he discovered that the youngsters on the books at Everton had to work at jobs other than kicking a football around. On the first day, it seemed as if things were going to be as he had expected – the lads were pitched into a practice match with the reserves, and Joe managed to score a goal. Then he got showered and changed, and prepared to set off for his home in Norris Green. It was at this point that he was made aware of what was expected of him. He was told that he hadn't quite finished, because he had to help in putting all the kit away and washing the dressing-room floors. The news came as a jolt, as he realised that he had to dirty his hands.

Every morning, it was a case of being down bright and early to do the chores: getting out the kit for training, cleaning boots and anything else which the trainers decided needed doing. And the young Joe Royle didn't endear himself to his superiors at that stage of his career, because he used to grumble about the jobs he was called upon to do – in fact, by his own admission, he tried to get away with doing as little as possible and he became known as a somewhat lazy lad. However, as time passed and he realised that the backroom men would not tolerate any shirking when it came to the chores, he also came to recognise that this was a kind of discipline which, in the long run, would do him no harm. So he buckled down to it, and on the football side he made real progress.

Right from the start it was made clear to him that Everton intended to groom him as a centre-forward. Gone were the days when he played right-half or centre-half; his job now was to lead the attack and stick the ball in the net, and, of course, he was well equipped physically to withstand any treatment a centre-half could dish out. During his first season he became a regular in Everton's 'B' team, and he produced 32 goals, which made him the team's top scorer. Even so, he still didn't relish his new position, and he really wished he could revert to playing at right-half. But his mentors kept on talking to him and insisting that he would find his niche as a centre-forward; and, in due course, he came to realise that this was a role which, at last, was giving him a genuine kick. Scoring goals was what it was all about.

Along the way, young Royle would find himself being pulled out of a practice match with the other kids and pitched into a session with the star names such as Alex Young and Brian Labone. The idea, of course, was to give him experience and increase his self-belief. It didn't take long for Joe Royle to break through to reserve-team football – he leap-frogged the 'A' team – and he stayed in the side right through the season. He was still just a teenager, and

Everton had plenty of big-name players on their books, so a first-team spot looked a considerable way off. But in the immediate future Joe Royle was to make headline news – and, in the final analysis, it wasn't the kind of news he would relish.

Chapter Four

DEBUT-DAY VENGEANCE!

It was recorded that Joe Royle's baptism as a First Division footballer led to 'one of the ugliest incidents in Everton's post-war history'. Joe himself has always tended to play things down, when I have talked to him about his debut at the tender age of 16, but I well recall that Everton's decision – or, rather, the decision of manager Harry Catterick – to throw him in at the deep end sparked off not only bitter controversy, but led to furious fans going for the manager. My recollection of the affair is that they ended up pinning Catterick against the side of the team coach and abusing him in no uncertain terms.

The date was 15 January 1966, and Harry Catterick had come to a big decision. He intended to give the 16-year-old Royle his senior debut in the important match against Blackpool at Bloomfield Road. Naturally, that in itself was headline material, because the lad would thus become the youngest centre-forward in First Division football; but fuel would be added to the fire in another respect. If Royle went in, it meant that someone had to drop out – and that someone, Harry Catterick decided, must be Alex Young, the Scotland international with the flaxen hair whom the Everton fans called the 'Golden Vision'. Young was a player of delicate artistry, a player with a silky touch as he led the front line and beat opposing goalkeepers. The young Joe

Royle was cast in a somewhat different mould. Where Young's frame was slender, Royle was a strapping lad who could match any centre-half in purely physical terms. Not quite a battering-ram, but not far from it.

The night before Joe Royle's debut, Catterick took Joe's father into his confidence, and what might be termed a security cordon was thrown around the teenager. The message was: 'We don't want the lad disturbed. The manager wants him to be kept as quiet as possible.' Joe was still three months short of his 17th birthday; he stood six foot three inches tall, weighed in at thirteen stone, and was described by his manager as 'a natural'. 'He can shoot with either foot and is the best header of a ball at the club. His progress has been remarkable. I don't care how he plays tomorrow or even this season. I have complete faith in him having the ability to become a first-class player.' Harry Catterick was indeed sticking his neck out – but the years that followed were to prove him correct in his assessment, as Joe Royle plundered a century of goals.

Young Joe's reaction to the news that he would be playing against Blackpool: 'I couldn't believe my ears when Mr Catterick told me I was in the first team. The words wouldn't sink in at first. I'm still in a bit of a daze. I wondered what was up when the boss sent for me to go to his office. The last thing I expected was to be told I was in the League side.' And, seemingly, that was just about the last thing the Everton faithful had expected, as well. Like Joe Royle, and Alex Young, no doubt, they were stunned by the news. So, even before the match itself, the arguments began, as the fans debated the wisdom – or the folly – of the manager in dispensing with the 'Golden Vision' and chucking young Royle into the conflict at Bloomfield Road.

With Alex Young sidelined, Joe found himself playing alongside two players who, between them, had cost £120,000. There was Fred Pickering, the £80,000 buy from Blackburn Rovers, and Alex Scott, signed from Glasgow

Rangers for £40,000. Joe Royle had played in 14 reserve-team matches by that time, and he had scored five goals; but did that mean he was good enough to stand comparison with a star like Alex Young? There was that old soccer saying: 'If they're good enough, then they're old enough' – but at the age of 16, young Royle had a man-sized job on his hands. For the Everton supporters there was the feeling that if Catterick had so much faith in Royle, what of the future at Everton for their hero, Alex Young? The writing must be on the wall for him.

Catterick's decision to sell Bobby Collins had caused some consternation among Everton's supporters, not least as they saw the chunky little 'pocket general' inspire Leeds United not only to promotion, but to the FA Cup final against Liverpool in 1965. Everton might have recouped their £25,000 outlay on the wee man, but the Goodison fans felt that he could still have done the business for their team. Now, here were signs that the career of Alex Young was taking a definite downward turn – and, for the most part, they didn't much care for that idea.

There was no real opposition to Joe Royle; after all, he was one of their own, Merseyside-born and bred. Come to that, he might well make his mark as a centre-forward in the mould of Dixie Dean and Tommy Lawton – but only in time. Right now, Everton's game at Blackpool wasn't the time or the place; and those fans who travelled to Bloomfield Road were even more convinced of this, at the final whistle. The pitch was bone-hard, which didn't help Everton's style of football; indeed, they failed to turn on anything like their true form, and their performance brought about their defeat, as Blackpool scored two goals without reply. The architect of Blackpool's victory was the flame-haired Alan Ball, a World Cup winner whom Harry Catterick, not long afterwards, was destined to take to Goodison Park. But, on that January day in 1966, the World Cup was still months away, and Ball was the enemy.

So, too, was Harry Catterick, in the eyes of the Everton supporters.

The young Royle found himself struggling in a struggling side, and for him it was more or less a non-event. Indeed, it was a bitter experience and a foretaste of the way that fans can be fickle and of the way that the game can bring troubles as well as trophies. For Everton's manager, it meant a rough ride as he was manhandled by the irate fans while trying to get aboard the team coach. After that match, Joe Royle was restored to reserve-team football, having admitted that he had made what he termed 'a poor contribution' to the Everton cause. What he remembered most was the way that Alan Ball ran the show for Blackpool. However, though Joe went back to the 'stiffs', he did get another chance to show his paces in the senior side that season.

This time out, he wasn't on his own, because Everton fielded no fewer than ten reserve-team players. They were on their way to the final of the FA Cup, and there could be no distractions – such as the League game against Don Revie's Leeds. There was one player in Everton's regular reserve-team line-up who got into the action against Leeds – Mike Trebilcock – and he was destined also to play a key role in the final against Sheffield Wednesday. That was another controversial decision which was made by Harry Catterick, and at one point it seemed as if he had made the wrong one.

In the meantime, Everton put out this team against Leeds United: Andy Rankin; Sandy Brown, Frank D'Arcy; John Hurst, Derek Smith, Gerry Glover; Jimmy Husband, Gerry Humphreys, Joe Royle, Mike Trebilcock, Johnny Morrissey. Everton's decision to field this second-string side brought a load of criticism down upon their heads, especially after Leeds had claimed victory by four goals to one (Trebilcock was Everton's marksman). The Football League inquired into matters and, in its wisdom, decided that Everton should be fined £2,000. The game against Leeds had come only seven days before the FA Cup semi-final against Manchester

United, and Everton's youngsters felt that they had not been disgraced, even though the scoreline appeared so decisive.

Harry Catterick (who had declared his first team unfit) seemingly remained unperturbed about the furore over his selection of the side to tackle Leeds; his sights, naturally, were on Wembley and winning the FA Cup. On that day, also, when Everton met his old club, Sheffield Wednesday, for a time Catterick once again became a target for the fans who followed the Blues; but, ultimately, as the result emphasised, his judgment and his team selection were vindicated.

Two years on, and Everton went back to Wembley, this time with Joe Royle playing up front. In the meantime, he kicked off his third season at Goodison Park once again as a reserve-team player, and the 17-year-old (as he was by that time) remained a regular until the later stages of the season. During the final weeks of the campaign, he was given his chance to demonstrate that, this time, he had fully earned his place, as he played in four of the club's last five League matches.

The following season, Royle had become recognised as Everton's centre-forward, as he nailed down the first-team spot on a regular basis. No doubt about it, he had arrived. And the match which finally clinched a place for him took place not at Goodison Park, not even on the ground of another League club in England, but on Irish soil, when Everton played Shamrock Rovers during the summer of 1967. Everton really turned on the style, and so did their teenage centre-forward, as he knocked in a couple of goals. It led to young Royle lining up in the first team when the new season got under way in earnest, and the opposition could not have been more glamorous – or testing – because it was provided by Manchester United. In United's side was Joe Royle's idol, Bobby Charlton; but it was Everton's young striker who enjoyed himself most, as his side scored a 3–1 victory in a thrilling match.

As the season progressed, so did Joe Royle. He found goals came along for him on a regular basis: in Everton's League matches, he was on the mark 16 times; in the FA Cup, he rattled in three more goals; and in the League Cup he was a marksman again. By the time the season ended, he had emerged as the club's joint top scorer, his partner being Alan Ball – whose 20 goals had all come in First Division games. Between them, the two strikers helped to ensure that Everton finished in fifth position, which was a reasonably satisfactory ending to the campaign, even though an appearance in the final of the FA Cup was destined to finish with young Royle and company walking up the steps as losers against West Brom. From a personal point of view, however, Everton's centre-forward could look back with some pleasure on the contribution he had made to his team's cause.

By then Joe had played in 33 League games, all the matches involving the FA Cup – including the final at Wembley – and he was an England Under-23 international. He had the ideal temperament for the big-time matches. He wasn't especially nervous before a game, as some players are; he could dish it out and take it on the field of play, without getting into trouble; and he could find the net with his head or with either foot. In short, he was a good all-round centre-forward. But when it came to the semi-finals of the FA Cup, for once he did find himself afflicted by nerves.

Joe always claimed that, indirectly, his 'FA Cup collywobbles', as he called them, led to Everton marching on to their Wembley date with West Bromwich Albion. And it boiled down to the question of which Everton player should take the penalties, if any were awarded during their semi-final against Leeds United at Old Trafford. Alan Ball, the regular penalty-taker, was suspended. When the verdict was announced, it was Joe Royle who had been given the job as Ball's spot-kick replacement, and the thought of this didn't appear to affect the young striker unduly – until the very eve

Howard Kendall: triumphs and trophies at home and in Europe, but the second time around became an unhappy experience

Gordon Lee: near-misses, as he took Everton to the semi-final of the FA Cup and the final of the League Cup

Billy Bingham: things didn't work out for him – or for Colin Harvey (centre) and Mike Walker

Above left: It's a derby game duel with Liverpool's Alec Lindsay, Chris Lawler and Tommy Smith closing in

Above right: Alan Ball, one of Everton's stars during the late 1960s, in action as Joe Royle (third from right) looks on

Left: Goal! And Arsenal keeper Bob Wilson can do nothing to prevent the ball from sailing into the net, as Alan Whittle – a marksman hero when Everton claimed the title in 1969–70 – savours the moment

Heads I win! Joe Royle rises to the occasion

Goalbound! Johnny Morrissey watches as the ball rockets past the keeper

Joe Royle (far right) and Alan Whittle know this ball is destined for the Stoke City net

*Lap of honour after the 1966 FA Cup-final victory over
Sheffield Wednesday*

*Champions! Manager Harry Catterick and his players savour the
success of season 1969–70*

Up for the Cup! Everton skipper Brian Labone receives the trophy from Princess Margaret while Gordon West awaits his turn to collect an FA Cup-winner's medal

Wembley again – and Everton's squad enjoy their FA Cup triumph in 1984 after victory over Watford

Men who wore the Everton jersey with distinction (clockwise from top left):
Duncan McKenzie, Alan Ball, Andy Gray and Brian Labone

of the game. Then, suddenly, nerves began to get a grip, and the more Joe thought about the prospect, the more uneasy he became. In the end, he asked to be relieved of the responsibility, and this was agreed. The job was passed on to Johnny Morrissey, and when Everton were awarded a penalty, the winger made no mistake.

As Morrissey stepped up to take aim, Joe Royle was saying a little prayer to himself, as he was honest enough to admit afterwards. 'I wouldn't have been in Johnny's shoes for anything in the world, at that moment,' he said. And, of course, there was the added worry that if Morrissey should miss, Joe might find his own team-mates blaming him for having ducked out. So there was double relief for the Everton striker when he saw the ball going past keeper Gary Sprake. In fact, Joe Royle had played his part in the goal in any event. Sprake was noted for his tendency to get a bit uptight on occasion, so Royle had been ordered to chivvy Sprake on his right-hand side whenever the keeper gathered the ball. The centre-forward did his job to such good effect that when he closed in Sprake did what Everton's manager had hoped he would: he switched to his left foot, which was the weaker of the two, and sent the ball straight out to Everton's winger, Jimmy Husband, who was just outside the 18-yard area. Husband, no mean striker of a ball, slammed it straight back, and big Jack Charlton, realising the danger, did the only thing he reckoned he could – he got his hand to the ball. Hence the penalty. Everton that day achieved their hard-fought win minus key players Ball and John Hurst; as for Joe Royle, he was on his way to Wembley at a time when he had only just turned 19.

Everton had disposed of Southport in the third round, but only after a struggle at homely Haig Avenue – a Kendall cross was nodded home by Royle, and it was the winner. Tranmere Rovers were next, at Goodison Park, and again a Royle header was on target, along with a goal from Morrissey. Joe did the trick again when Everton went to Brunton Park and beat Carlisle United 2–0, after Husband scored only seconds into the game. A Kendall pass reached Everton's centre-forward on the halfway line, and Joe left one defender after another in his wake as he headed for goal. As keeper Alan Ross advanced, Royle drove the ball low into the left-hand corner, and Carlisle knew that their dreams of Cup glory had been shattered.

The quarter-final brought First Division opposition in the shape of Leicester City, and although the tie was played at Filbert Street, Everton really turned on the style – they scored three times to Leicester's once, with Husband notching a couple of goals and Kendall completing the job. Then it was Leeds in the semi-final, and on to Wembley to meet West Brom – which proved, indeed, to be a big let-down for Everton and their supporters. Oddly enough, West Brom had dashed hopes of an all-Merseyside final by knocking out Liverpool while Everton were disposing of Leeds. Yet Everton were the Wembley favourites, since they had hammered West Brom 2–0 at The Hawthorns only a matter of weeks before. Once again they outplayed the Albion, but they couldn't translate territorial superiority into goals, and when Jeff Astle struck, with a shot which went home like a bullet, that was the beginning and the end of the scoring. Joe Royle saw a shot cleared off the line by John Kay, after the keeper had been beaten, but a near-miss wasn't enough.

Royle and company may have been very disappointed by that Wembley result, but they were heading for Championship success not long afterwards; and the composition of the team showed just how the changes had been rung since the club had captured the title trophy at the end of season 1962–63. Then, the side usually read like this: West; Parker, Thomson; Gabriel, Labone, Kay; Bingham, Scott, Young, Vernon, Temple. Bobby Collins had just departed for Leeds, and Colin Harvey was on the point of making his European debut and forcing his way through to the senior side on a regular basis. Even so, Harry Catterick was looking five years ahead, and working on reinforcing his squad with big-money signings and home-produced talent.

One player he signed was Sandy Brown, a Scottish footballer who could operate in several roles, and it was a measure of Catterick's thoroughness that even as the club was celebrating a Championship success, the manager was vanishing and taking the high road for Scotland, without telling a soul. While players and club officials wined and dined in a swish Liverpool hotel, Catterick got into his car, changed from evening dress into a lounge suit, and drove through the night, having just learned that Brown, of Partick Thistle, was available. By 8.30 the next morning, he was waiting outside Partick's Firhill ground for manager Willie Thornton to arrive, and a deal was struck at £22,000. Brown at that time was playing at left-back, but he demonstrated that he could adapt to other positions as he became Everton's Mr Versatile. He switched to right-back, centre-half, centre-forward and even, on one occasion, did a stint as emergency goalkeeper. Finally, when Ramon Wilson, one of England's World Cup heroes, was bowing out, Sandy nailed down the No. 3 spot.

The Everton team which won the FA Cup in 1966 differed from that which had claimed the Championship. Now it read: West; Wright, Wilson; Gabriel, Labone, Harris; Scott, Trebilcock, Young, Harvey, Temple. Billy Bingham, Alex Parker, George Thomson, Tony Kay and Roy Vernon were no longer a part of the Goodison scene – Kay, indeed, had fallen foul of the authorities, while Vernon had moved on to Stoke City. Vernon, in fact, was the reason that John Moores fell out with me.

Royston Vernon hailed from a little village in North Wales called Ffynongroew, and he was one of football's most ebullient characters. I got to know him well, and quickly came to recognise that he had a lively sense of humour and could be a bit of a practical joker. On the pitch he feared no one, and he had a razor-sharp brain which took him into scoring positions and enabled him to get goals. He had a lean frame and a good turn of speed – all this, despite the fact that he used to enjoy puffing away at a cigarette. It was said that before a game he would do a disappearing act into the toilet, and that wisps of smoke could be seen coming from the cubicle. Roy Vernon, despite his quirky humour, was never malicious . . . Sadly, he died at the age of 56, after having returned to Blackburn, where he had first made his name in football. When he joined Stoke, he told manager Tony Waddington: 'I'm the best signing you'll ever make . . .' But in truth, his career blossomed during his time at Everton.

Tony Kay, another ebullient character, was, like Alan Ball, a red-head – bouncy, too, and full of confidence. Like Roy Vernon, he enjoyed a smoke – in his case, he usually sported a cigar, as well as a cheeky smile. He had come to prominence with Sheffield Wednesday during Harry Catterick's time there as team boss, and Catterick had no hesitation in taking him to Goodison Park as Wednesday received a consolation fee of £55,000. It was the paper on which I worked, *The People*, which landed Kay and two Wednesday players, Peter Swan and David 'Bronco' Layne, in deep trouble. Reporter Mike Gabbert spent a long time delving into things, but he came up with a story which, to put it mildly, staggered football. The end product was that Kay, Layne and Swan, along with seven others, appeared on charges of conspiracy to defraud by 'fixing' the results of matches, and prison sentences were passed when the ten professional and former professional players wound up at Nottingham Assizes in January 1965. So ended Tony Kay's career with Everton and England – like Swan, he had been capped by his country, and he was rated one of the most tenacious wing-halves in the game. It was a sad and sorry story which unfolded, first in *The People*, and then in the courtroom. All three players were suspended *sine die*, although the suspensions on Swan and Layne were lifted in 1972.

By the time Everton had faced up to West Brom at Wembley, the composition of the side had undergone more changes. It was still West in goal, Wright and Wilson at full-back; but the half-back line now read Kendall, Labone, Harvey; and the front line consisted of Husband, Ball, Royle, Hurst and Morrissey, with Roger Kenyon named as substitute. Howard Kendall had become the youngest player to appear in an FA Cup final when, at the age of 17 (20 days before his 18th birthday), he had been in the line-up for Preston North End against West Ham. That was in 1964, and before long he had been snapped up by Harry Catterick for Everton, at a fee of £80,000. It was a typical smash-and-grab raid by Harry for a player who, originally, hadn't even been in Preston's Wembley squad. But three days before the final, Preston sensationally axed left-half Ian Davidson after a breach of club discipline and, suddenly, Kendall was in.

When Catterick swooped, he pipped Bill Shankly for North End's young starlet. Liverpool had been first in with a bid for him and they, like everyone else, were shaken when the 20-year-old Kendall put pen to paper for Everton in March 1967. He went straight into the side at No. 4, to link with Harvey and Ball and forge that famous partnership. By the time Everton and Kendall were going to Wembley in 1968, Catterick's revamped team had taken shape for a third time. Yet not all the players were expensive acquisitions. Brian Labone, like Tommy Wright, Colin Harvey, Jimmy Husband, John Hurst and Joe Royle, had been home-grown, while Johnny Morrissey had played for Liverpool before moving 'across the park' for a modest fee. He, too, was a Liverpudlian born and bred, as was Roger Kenyon, the substitute centre-half, while John Hurst, although from the Blackpool area, had not cost Everton a fee and had been on the club's books while still a youngster.

Jimmy Gabriel had joined Southampton, Brian Harris had gone to Cardiff City, Alex Scott had returned north of the border, Mike Trebilcock had moved back down south to

Portsmouth, and Derek Temple had joined Preston. Alex Young was still around at Goodison Park, but his days there were fast drawing to a close. Everton had had full money's worth from every player, and they were to get this kind of value not only from Sandy Brown, but from local lad Alan Whittle, who showed he could turn games by scoring vital goals. Catterick also took on board more big names – players such as Keith Newton and Henry Newton. As for Joe Royle, he was now being tipped to figure in England's World Cup squad for Mexico. By that time, young Joe had come up against the very best that the First Division could offer in the shape of centre-halves, and he had demonstrated that he need not fear any of them – though this didn't prevent him from having great respect for the likes not only of his team-mate, Brian Labone, but for Liverpool's 'Colossus', Ron Yeats, and that elegant defender at Tottenham Hotspur, Mike England (who was later to manage the Wales international side). According to Joe, these three were the best centre-halves he had encountered; and this was not surprising.

I have one outstanding memory concerning Mike England, and not from a game of football; it stemmed from the days when he was playing for Blackburn Rovers, and I ran a story forecasting that he would shortly be transferred to Tottenham Hotspur. At that time, the Rovers had a very fair side indeed – Ronnie Clayton, Bryan Douglas and so on – and they seemed to be candidates for a trophy. But, as ever in those days, money was the root of the problem (Jack Walker hadn't appeared on the scene) and so it looked inevitable that England would go. On the Sunday morning that the story appeared in *The People*, Rovers manager Jack Marshall phoned me at home to register a plaintive plea. Usually, people referred to him as 'Jolly Jack', because he was rarely without a smile on his face, and he and I got on well together. But on this occasion, he was ringing to ask me: 'What are you trying to do?' And, in the same breath, he was telling me: 'Here am I, trying to keep a team together, and I waken up to read that Mike England's going to Tottenham.' I told him that I had run the story in good faith, and that I truly believed the event would happen; it did, indeed, as England travelled south to sign for Spurs and the Rovers pocketed another, much-needed fee. Needless to say, they did not win the Championship or any other trophy that season.

If Jolly Jack Marshall had his problems at Blackburn, Joe Royle had to face up to the possibility of losing his place in the first team at Everton, because there came a time when the newspapers were full of reports that the Goodison Park club was in the bidding for Scottish striker Colin Stein. He had first made his name with Hibernian, then joined Rangers and became a £100,000 centre-forward. Now the talk was that he would join Everton.

Royle had been having something of a lean spell finding the net and, as he admitted, he came to the conclusion that if he didn't pull up his socks he could find himself out of favour. The transfer talk about Stein didn't help matters, either. In the first week of November 1968 Everton met Ipswich Town at Portman Road. That match ended in a 2–2 draw, but Joe Royle had every reason to be happy about the result. He had headed both his side's goals to restore his own confidence and silence his critics, if only for the time being. That draw kept Everton going neck and neck with Liverpool at the top of the First Division, and there was more to come as the season unfolded.

One of Joe's goals against Ipswich was rated 'a shade lucky', and the other was classed as 'clever'; no matter, as Royle well knew, they all counted. It was recorded: 'There was a Championship quality in the way Everton made something out of nothing to draw a match they had looked like winning hands down. But would-be champions out of the right mould don't droop like wilting tulips when a match tips away from them. Everton must become big enough to roll – perhaps reel – under impact, but not sag. To justify their rating as title contenders, they must also resist trying to catch up through testy personal tactics usually associated with desperate Fourth Division sides. Only 23,000 turned out to see the League leaders, 7,000 fewer than Spurs attracted last month. Ipswich fans must have guessed. For eight minutes Everton looked fully competent. When Royle leapt tremendously to reach a high cross from Morrissey and sent a header dipping under the bar, Everton had it made.' But Ipswich came back and the result was a 2–2 draw. Everton could have reminded that particular critic, at a later stage, that not only did they win the Championship in 1969–70 but that they did it in such style that they proved worthy of the honour, as they almost equalled the Leeds United record feat of totalling 67 points. But, of course, they still had some way to go in season 1968–69; although for Joe Royle, it was a season which saw him come good.

Three weeks after his two-goal salvo at Portman Road, Royle was hitting his first-ever hat-trick in First Division football, as Everton set about hapless Leicester City and gave them a good hiding at Goodison Park. The final score was 7–1, and the hat-trick took Royle's tally of goals for the season (it was then still only late November) to 17. It took his overall score to 33 goals in 60 First Division outings and, of course, it helped in no small measure to banish all talk of Colin Stein taking Royle's No. 9 jersey from him.

Joe gave considerable credit to Alan Ball for his welcome return to the goal standard. Together, they had put in extra training stints aimed at working up a closer understanding; they had discussed tactics, talked over how they could link up more successfully; and it all came right in the match against Leicester City. Remarkably, while Manchester City despatched Everton from the FA Cup in the semi-final that season, lowly Leicester also managed to make it all the way to Wembley. There they lost out to a goal by Neil Young – and they lost out, too, in the League, as they suffered the indignity of relegation.

Meanwhile, just in case Joe Royle should start getting ideas above his station, Ball, with typical candour, made sure Everton's centre-forward kept his feet firmly on the ground. Ball offered due praise to his team-mate while, at the same time, tempering the praise with this comment: 'He is not over-great on the floor, but there's time for improvement in that direction.' And Brian Labone also contributed some sage advice, as he told Joe: 'It's up to you to keep it up – you must continue to get that little bit extra out of your game.' Labone was a down-to-earth character who never considered himself to be a star; indeed, he was the epitome of the team player. And, of course, Joe was just grateful that things had started to go his way again when it came to scoring goals. A commentator on the Merseyside soccer scene summed it up: 'What a revelation is this man Royle, so hesitant and lacking confidence earlier in the season. He must be among the most improved footballers in the country. Instead of being an Everton worry, he is now a hero, and a man they look towards in their lofty ambitions.'

Joe carried on where he had left off, when Everton travelled to Sunderland, scoring twice in their 3–1 victory at Roker Park (both goals came from headers) and after that match he was totting up his score again, with the tally working out at 38 goals in 70 League appearances. Twenty-one of those goals had come during season 1968–69, and ten of them had been from headers. Joe then set his sights on collecting 30 goals altogether by the time the season ended. Yet there were one or two occasions when he had to break through the pain barrier to hit the target – for example, just before the brace of goals which kept Everton in the race for the Championship, with that victory over Sunderland, the young striker had been in absolute agony. He had been to the dentist in midweek to have a tooth extracted, and for the next four days his life had been a misery. He had been taking up to a dozen pain-killers a day, had missed a day's training, and was far from fit when he lined up against Sunderland.

This, of course, is the kind of thing the fans never stop to consider when they see a player unable to turn on his best form – they simply criticise every mistake even though the player is doing his best. In Royle's case at Roker Park, he was suffering from an abscess and, as he said later: 'I felt as though I had a cricket ball in my mouth.' He also acknowledged that his work-rate suffered during the second half – but those two goals did provide some kind of tonic for him. And, of course, in due time he recovered, to carry on finding the net. When it came to the FA Cup, in fact, he was a marksman in every round, barring one – the semi-final which Everton lost against Manchester City.

Bristol Rovers provided an extremely tough contest when they went to Goodison Park for the fifth round of the Cup, and it was Royle who became the match-winner as he crashed home a tremendous shot. He was on the mark again, this time as Everton went to Old Trafford and despatched Manchester United from the competition. After that winning goal, he was described as 'the kid with the KO punch'. The goal came via a corner kick from Johnny Morrissey which was flicked on by Jimmy Husband into the middle. As centre-half Steve James failed to intercept, Joe Royle – seemingly startled by the sudden opportunity which was presented – had a go. Initially, he knocked the ball with his knee, but followed through and found the net.

Everton's victory was accomplished without the injured Kendall, while Harvey managed to stay on the park for no more than 55 minutes – he, too, became a casualty. However, when it came to the semi-final against Manchester City, things didn't turn out the way Everton wanted, because Joe Mercer's team put paid to visions of another trip to Wembley. Ironically, Mercer himself had once upon a time been an idol of the fans at Goodison Park; and another of those soccer twists and turns was to see Joe Royle going to Wembley with Manchester City, to collect a winner's medal in the League Cup competition. But that day when

Manchester City defeated Everton in the FA Cup semi-final, the hero for Joe Mercer's team was one Franny Lee, who became chairman of the Maine Road club during the mid-1990s. Royle admired Lee as much as he admired his own team-mate, Alan Ball, and all three players won their share of honours before they moved on – in Royle's case, when he finally packed his bags as a player at Goodison Park, his travels were to take him to Manchester, Bristol and Norwich before he embarked upon management with Oldham Athletic.

Chapter Five

CATTERICK'S COMPLAINT

In much the same way that Manchester United were said to have let the Championship slip from their grasp, when they were pipped at the post by Leeds United in 1991–92, so Leeds were said to have allowed Everton to wrest the title from them during season 1969–70. Manchester United, by their own admission, did indeed allow Leeds to snatch the prize at the death; but Everton – despite any failings Don Revie's team might have had – won the Championship for themselves, and there cannot be the slightest doubt about the merit of their triumph. Like Manchester United and Blackburn Rovers in 1994–95, Everton and Leeds slogged it out in a tug-o'-war for the title during 1969–70 and, when the final drama unfolded, it was Everton who had their noses in front.

Along the way Everton, hampered by injuries, responded to the challenge in such sterling fashion that they amassed 66 points (Leeds totalled 57). Leeds, during their record-breaking season, lost only two League games and Don Revie told me later: 'One day another club might equal our points total [67], but I doubt if any other club will better our record of two defeats.' Everton went so close on points, although they did suffer five defeats – but they ended Leeds' record unbeaten sequence along the way. Leeds had gone 34 games, spanning seasons 1968–69 and 1969–70; but on 30 August

1969 their run was halted as they went to Goodison Park and lost 3–2. The Leeds sequence had consisted of 19 victories and 15 draws. Apart from winning that game, the fact that Everton finished no fewer than nine points ahead of Leeds was no mean feat in itself.

The season kicked off with Everton going great guns. They went through their first seven games without defeat, and in the process they collected 13 points out of 14. When faced with accusations that it was Leeds who had allowed Everton to slip into the driving seat, Catterick and his players could counter, with perfect truth, that this argument simply didn't hold water. The facts spoke for themselves: when it came to the last nine matches, Everton went through them as they had gone through their first seven, picking up 17 points out of the possible 18. That was more than Championship form, and it showed just how well Everton had managed to keep their nerve.

In between what could be termed those two purple patches of form, Everton had had problems. Brian Labone was out injured for quite some time and had to be replaced by Sandy Brown. On top of that, they had had to make do without Colin Harvey for a lengthy spell; and they had lost Alan Ball for five weeks, because he had been suspended. There was a credit side, though: a youngster – a local lad at that – by the name of Alan Whittle was pitched into the side, and he began to rifle home goals which brought Everton quite a number of their points. When it came to the crucial Easter matches, Leeds United were beaten twice and it was said that those defeats cost them the title. Even had Leeds not lost, they would still have finished second, because at the death they totalled 57 points to Everton's 66.

True enough, Everton suffered a spell during September that season – it was described as 'a wobble' – when they struggled to maintain their momentum and slipped from the top into third place, but for the most part they were the leaders and, in fact, at one stage during October they were ahead by the handsome margin of eight points. When the mudheap grounds began to take their toll on the lightweights, Leeds United started to exert their power as Christmas and the New Year came into focus. In mid-January, Everton travelled to The Dell and were beaten 2–1 by Southampton, and so Leeds United took over at the top with such an air of confidence that the Everton faithful began to feel a little dismayed.

That, indeed, was Everton's lowest point of the campaign. They had gone to Elland Road and suffered defeat, they had been knocked out of the FA Cup by another Yorkshire club, Sheffield United. And to add to their problems, Alan Ball had just commenced his five-week suspension. There was a kind of consolation prize, in that Colin Harvey had recovered from his injury, and he came back into the side. Even so, the pressure upon Everton was increasing, and when they went to the City Ground and drew, 1–1, against Nottingham Forest, there was a nodding of heads in some quarters. Goalkeeper Gordon West recalled that game as we talked one day, shortly after the title trophy had been won and lost. 'We had desperately needed the tonic of a win – and the bonus of two points – to edge us nearer to the title,' he said. 'In the dressing-room after the match, the lads were a bit quiet, and I could sense that Harry Catterick was also wishing we'd been able to nail down both points – although we weren't turning our noses up at the one we'd got. I was feeling like everyone else; that while we'd done all right, we hadn't done quite well enough. Then the boss turned to me and said, "Great save you made, son, in those last few minutes." It dawned on me then that we could all have been returning to Goodison empty-handed.'

West then told me how the save had come about. 'Forest won a corner and the ball came over. Their full-back, Peter Hindley, had come up and he sent in a bullet-like header – it had "goal" written all over it. The ball was flying towards the top corner, and how I got there I'll never know – it was purely a reflex action. But I flicked the ball over the bar.'

Of course, the ball had gone for another corner, and this time the danger was cleared, just in time for the referee to blow his whistle and put an end to the suspense. So, as West said, if Everton hadn't won, they had averted a defeat in those dying minutes. And they pulled up their socks after this let-off by going to Turf Moor and, on a snow-capped, slippery pitch, they scored a 2–1 victory over Burnley. So they came through their bleak spell when they were hanging on grimly, just managing to keep in touch with Leeds. That win at Burnley boosted Everton's confidence, and they started to feel that the title race was still there to be won – if they could keep their nerve.

Alan Ball and John Hurst had scored the goals at Burnley, and that success took Everton on to 51 points. It was then that Alan Whittle, a blond-haired youngster with the golden touch, began a sequence of scoring which had the Leeds United fans wondering if Everton had produced a winner. At the third time of asking, Everton and Tottenham Hotspur managed to complete their fixture at White Hart Lane (the weather had caused the first postponement, then a floodlight failure had halted the second encounter). It was Whittle who slotted home the decisive goal and Everton had picked up two more points.

Spurs then had to visit Goodison Park three days later in what turned out to be a five-goal thriller, with Everton finally just having the edge. Everton were back on top, and at Goodison there were more than 51,500 raucous voices to cheer this victory which gave the Blues a three-point lead over Leeds. According to Harry Catterick, 'we are just beginning to tick again'. That Saturday, which saw Everton defeat Spurs, Leeds United had embarked upon what turned out to be a marathon FA Cup duel with Manchester United – it was the semi-final stage – and although the Champions now had a match in hand, they also had to face Celtic in the semi-finals of the European Cup. Tough on Leeds, of course, but that's the kind of price you have to pay when you're having so much success. From Everton's point of view, the more distractions for Leeds, the better for Everton. Even so, the Goodison outfit were well aware that nothing could be taken for granted, at this late stage of the season. The remaining matches still had to be won.

This task was accomplished in genuine style, not least when Everton crossed Stanley Park to do battle with Liverpool at Anfield. In December, Liverpool had shaken Harry Catterick's men – and Everton's fans – by going to Goodison Park and inflicting a defeat upon the Blues. This time it was Everton's turn to go home laughing, as Whittle and Royle scored the goals which brought a 2–0 victory. Meanwhile, Leeds United had beaten Wolves at Molineux but they still had to meet Manchester United in their FA Cup replay. That one ended in another draw, and the next game saw Leeds going to Burnden Park to tackle United yet again. By Good Friday, Leeds, 1–0 winners in their second replay, were through to Wembley, and both they and Everton could be grateful for small mercies – on that icy day, on the eve of the Easter weekend, they were not being called upon to engage in a soccer lottery. Even so, for Leeds there was the worry of having several casualties, after their semi-final joust with Manchester United.

On Easter Saturday, it was Chelsea (who were due to meet Leeds shortly in the final at Wembley) at Goodison Park, and the sun shone as if to point the way home for Everton. If the sky was blue, however, the wind was blowing as if it came straight from the Arctic. But Everton went out and turned on a performance which left the Cup finalists stopped in their tracks. It was an awesome display of pace, power and pure skill. Howard Kendall struck Everton's first goal in 15 seconds, and Alan Ball headed home a second only a few minutes later. In the second half, Everton lost John Hurst for a spell (he had suffered a head injury); but this handicap didn't seem to matter, as Everton rammed home three more goals, even though Chelsea did manage to score twice themselves in the closing stages of the game.

In a matter of days, the Championship pendulum had tilted Everton's way with a vengeance. It meant that no matter what Leeds United did in the closing stages, so long as Everton walked off the Goodison pitch with two points from their game against West Bromwich Albion on the Wednesday night, they could not be caught. Everton duly scored a couple of goals which ensured that the title trophy returned to Goodison Park for the second time in seven years under the management of Harry Catterick. As for Leeds United, they could look back on that devastating home defeat by Southampton. As the goals went into their net, it was termed 'the worst 25 minutes since Don Revie took over as manager'.

It was after that match that Revie virtually conceded the Championship race had been won and lost, because he arranged for his team to play West Ham on the following Thursday, giving them an almost impossible League schedule. And when Leeds went down 4–1 at Derby, they fielded what amounted to a reserve side (their action resulted in them being fined £5,000). So, clearly, they had their sights on the consolation prize of the FA Cup. At that stage, Everton led the way by seven points, and Leeds faced up to the fact that it was a hopeless chase. In the end, Leeds won nothing. They outplayed Chelsea at Wembley, and I was at Old Trafford for the midweek replay. It was a game in which, once more, Chelsea appeared to be heading for defeat until David Webb scored the winner which stunned Don Revie and his players.

The Championship? The Football League had decreed in its wisdom that the trophy would not be presented; but then there was a change of heart, and so the scene was set for the title triumph as Everton despatched West Brom at Goodison Park. Manchester United chairman Louis Edwards was a spectator, and afterwards he presented the glittering trophy to the new champions. The match itself was played on a cold night; not long before the kick-off, the fans were drenched and chilled by a shower of sleet which lasted all of 20 minutes. But there was no taking away the warm glow of satisfaction they felt as Everton beat West Brom. Alan Whittle struck his sixth goal in as many matches, after a somewhat nervous start by the home side. Joe Royle and John Hurst each drilled efforts against the post, and Colin Harvey struck to settle both nerves and the title issue. That was the signal for the crowd of more than 58,500 to go wild.

Everton's chairman at the time, Jack Sharp, admitted that while 'we always felt we could win it this season. Leeds had taken on so much – but we felt we could match them, player for player. Even when we lost Harvey and Ball, and faltered a little, there was never any lack of confidence. We felt we could win the Championship in our own right.' Harry Catterick was typically restrained as he said: 'They wanted me to predict this success weeks ago, but I have learned to be patient. I rate this a tremendous achievement to score 28 wins in this, the greatest competition in the world.'

Everton still had two matches to play, and both were away: against struggling Sheffield Wednesday and Sunderland. There were suspicions of offside as Johnny Morrissey scored the goal which won the match at Hillsborough (the home fans had vented their displeasure over this one; maybe there was a touch of resentment, also, because Harry Catterick had once been Wednesday's manager). At Roker Park, Everton had to settle for a share of the points, and so they finished with their total of 66, one behind that record tally achieved by Leeds. Everton's seventh Championship put them level with Arsenal, Liverpool and Manchester United.

Looking back, they could claim that everyone in the squad had turned up trumps – not least Sandy Brown and Roger Kenyon, who had stood in when injuries took their toll. As for the goals, those from Alan Whittle had been worth quite a few precious points, while Tommy Wright and Joe Royle had been match-winners – Royle's goal had ensured two points at Coventry in the closing seconds. Alan Ball, too, had won the Goodison game against Derby County with his lone goal. Even had Leeds United not been facing so many games in three competitions, it is doubtful if they could have improved upon Everton's winning streak. Their captain, the irrepressible Alan Ball, made this prediction: 'This is the start of five great years for Everton.' How wrong can you be?

That Championship triumph turned out to be the pinnacle not only for Everton's manager, but for several of his players. Alan Ball, for instance, who, instead of enjoying 'five great years' with Everton, found himself becoming expendable as Catterick decided that an offer from Arsenal was just too good to refuse. And, indeed, it was, because after the sterling service Ball had rendered to the Goodison club, he went to Highbury for a transfer fee of £115,000, which meant that Everton had made a profit of £5,000 on a player who had given them around half a dozen seasons. Joe Royle, also, was not too far off the point of departure; he didn't know it then, but he was due to pack his boots and travel some 30 miles down the East Lancashire road to play for the Blues at Manchester City. By the time he left Goodison Park, Harry Catterick's term as manager had ended and another one-time Everton player, Billy Bingham, had taken charge of team affairs.

Chapter Six

A MANAGER'S JINX

Everton's Championship success of season 1969–70 came immediately before England's World Cup excursion to Mexico, and three Everton players – Gordon West, Brian Labone and Joe Royle – were looking likely lads for Alf Ramsey's squad. In the event, West declared his hand by informing Ramsey in advance not to consider him for the World Cup; Labone had already decided to turn his back upon soccer (and been persuaded to reverse that decision); and Joe Royle, who postponed his plans to marry Janet Hughes, found himself being put on stand-by but not being called up for the trip to Mexico.

West, in fact, had made up his mind to quit the international scene even before Everton had outrun Leeds United in the race for the Championship trophy, and he wrote to tell Ramsey of his decision. 'I know some folk thought I was daft, turning down such an opportunity – and, believe me, it wasn't an easy decision to make,' he said later. 'I'd won three caps, was still only in my mid-20s – but, when it came down to it, I knew I didn't want to go on a soccer safari which would take me away from home for something like ten weeks. I'd been with England on a close-season trip to South America, so I'd had a foretaste of what it was like, and I'd come to the conclusion that I would get soccer-weary. "Have boots, will travel" . . . that just wasn't me.' So West opted out.

Like Gordon West, Brian Labone was to feel the pressures of being a top-rank footballer; a player of whom Matt Busby had said: 'He looks to have a bright international future.' Labone had taken over from Tommy Jones, one of the Everton fans' heroes, in January 1960. Jones switched to full-back and Labone began a sequence of 66 matches. Labone's career had really kicked off with a game against Dave Hickson (noted for his dashing style of centre-forward play) in a public practice match and, after he had achieved first-team recognition, Labby went from strength to strength. But in September 1965 he was dropped for the first time and, to the surprise of many, he admitted with total candour that 'I think the manager is right when he picks me, so I can only agree with his judgment now he has dropped me'. Not many players would say that.

However, Labone fought his way back and became rated as a very close rival to Jack Charlton, whom Ramsey made his first choice in 1966. But, like Gordon West, Everton's defender showed his hand when he found himself being called up for a World Cup warm-up. Four days after being asked to replace Chelsea's Marvin Hinton in the squad, Labone announced that he intended to put his wedding date before any summons for World Cup duty. And in the autumn of 1966, Everton were shattered when Labone revealed his intention to quit football in 18 months' time. He was 28, and he summed up: 'I finally decided the pressure is just too much. You have no idea what the tension has been like – not physical, but mental. You would think that after 300 League games I would have got over it, but it has become worse with success. These days Everton have such a fabulous team you feel they should win every game. When they don't, you torture yourself thinking it is your fault.'

Labone knew he could go into the family business – 'I've always had that security behind me, and you would think that would help me to relax and enjoy my football. But I can't help worrying. I play in an important position, and before every game my stomach is churning so badly I feel ill. Soccer is a wonderful way of life, but no matter how big and hard a business football has become, to me it is still a game. There is no possibility of my playing again for another club. To me, there is only one club – Everton.' Then, to everyone's relief, he changed his mind and agreed to stay on, saying: 'When I decided to retire, the tension drained away from me.' And so he played an important part through much of Everton's Championship season of 1969–70 (except for the final seven games, when he was injured).

Everton hadn't quite come to the end of their bid for glory under Harry Catterick's management, at the start of the 1970s, because they went to the semi-finals of the FA Cup in season 1970–71, only to come up against Liverpool. It was a dramatic affair, although Everton's manager was conspicuous by his absence – he had fallen victim to a flu bug and was confined to his bed. The match started promisingly enough, as Everton swept into the lead with a goal from Alan Ball. Bill Shankly's side was in a transitional stage, with Ray Clemence having replaced Tommy Lawrence in goal, and newcomers in Steve Heighway and Brian Hall still finding their feet at the top level. They also had Alun Evans, the first £100,000 teenager, and John Toshack, signed from Cardiff City for £110,000.

Then tragedy struck; and Everton were the ones who were made to suffer as Labone, their lynch-pin at centre-half, pulled a hamstring and was helped off, limping. For him, the Cup-tie was over; and for Everton it was the beginning of the end. Although Sandy Brown was switched into the middle of the defence and as usual contributed 100 per cent, you sensed that Everton's cause had been damaged. So it proved. Shankly gave his troops a half-time pep-talk and, as he told me after the final whistle: 'We were banging the ball upfield and by-passing our midfielders – they would have needed step-ladders to get to the ball.' So Liverpool changed their tactics on the restart, and Tommy

Smith was the epitome of their herculean efforts to gain control. Afterwards, Shankly was moved to say of Smith: 'It will be a disgrace if he doesn't play for England; he's not just a hard man – he can play fitba', too.' (Indeed, he could, and he did play for England.) Liverpool went for an equaliser and then a winner. They succeeded on both counts, through Evans and Hall.

When I reached the dressing-room after the match, Shankly was holding court. The Everton players came out of their dressing-room, looking disconsolate and close to tears, not least because they had been beaten by the old enemy. When I recalled that sad day to Joe Royle, after his return to Goodison as manager, he reflected: 'When I look back, I feel I should have switched to centre-half to deal with the threat from Toshack – although, of course, it's easy to be wise after the event. But I had started out as a centre-half, remember, and I had the height to deal with the aerial danger from Tosh. I think I might have made a difference to Everton.'

As time went on, Ball was transferred to Arsenal, Howard Kendall to Birmingham, Joe Royle to Manchester City, and Harry Catterick finally came to the end of his tenure as the manager at Goodison Park. All these events came to pass in the course of a comparatively short time, and Everton were to hire half a dozen team bosses before they and their supporters could celebrate success again, this time at home *and* abroad. Even then it was a close-run thing for a while. The next manager, after Catterick, was another former player, Billy Bingham. I attended the press conference to announce his appointment officially and made a point of having a few words with him and wishing him success as Everton's new manager. His career the second time around at Goodison didn't end on a high note, although he made some notable signings. One newcomer was Bruce Rioch, whom Bingham recruited from Derby County, and another was Duncan McKenzie, whose travels took him from Nottingham Forest to Leeds United, on to Belgian football with Anderlecht, and also to Chelsea and Blackburn, as well as to Everton. In fact, I played a small part in the deal which took Duncan from Stamford Bridge to Ewood Park, because after the clubs had agreed terms, the player-manager negotiations took place in my home, on a Saturday morning.

McKenzie, of course, was a player in the Everton mould, and he had been signed by Brian Clough for Leeds United – then found that, after only 44 days in charge, Clough was on his way. Now, at Everton, McKenzie was paraded at a press conference, Bingham having told him when they first got down to business that: 'The side badly needs a lift.' Everton, indeed, had been going through a spell where results were not forthcoming, and along with a dip in morale there had been a drop in attendances. Bingham clearly hoped that McKenzie and Rioch, two expensive imports, would bring about a change in fortunes.

As Bingham and McKenzie posed for pictures – the television cameras were at Goodison, as well as the press photographers – the manager stood with one arm around Duncan's shoulder and, in what seemed at the time to be a jocular aside, he told his new recruit: 'The last time a manager signed you, he got the sack a couple of weeks later!' That, of course, was a reference to what had happened to Clough – and a few weeks after McKenzie arrived at Everton, the Goodison club was dispensing with the services of Billy Bingham.

So it was farewell Billy and, in January 1977, all hail to Gordon Lee, a down-to-earth manager who had been persuaded to leave Blackburn Rovers for Newcastle United, and who was now expected to bring Everton success. Lee had steered the Rovers to promotion and was to take Everton to a League Cup final, but at Newcastle he had earned a reputation as a manager who reckoned nothing to the so-called star system, and he had aroused a furore among the Geordie fans when he sold Malcolm Macdonald to Arsenal.

The manner of Billy Bingham's departure came as something of a surprise to Everton's players, because they had just turned on a very good performance to dispose of Stoke City in the third round of the FA Cup. On McKenzie's arrival, he had been able (as he told me later) to sense that the atmosphere in the dressing-room was 'a bit low', and it appeared to him as if the other players were, as Billy Bingham had indicated, expecting Bruce Rioch and himself to give them a lift. However, when Everton met Coventry City in icy conditions at Highfield Road, the result was a bad one for the men from Goodison Park. The final scoreline read: Coventry City 4, Everton 2. Still, Bingham seemed to feel that his players had put up an improved performance.

The next match was at home against Birmingham City, and naturally the players were feeling rather anxious about the outcome. They had reasonable cause to be happy at the final whistle, however, because they shared four goals – and McKenzie had got off to a flying start with the home supporters because he scored both Everton goals. Then came the turn of the year and with it the third round of the FA Cup. Everton's luck was in when they were paired with Stoke City at Goodison Park. According to McKenzie, it was probably Everton's best performance since he had arrived at the club, and they recorded a 2–0 win over Stoke.

Even so, 48 hours before the Cup-tie, there were dressing-room rumours to the effect that Bingham's job was on the line and, 48 hours after the Cup victory, the rumours became fact. It did seem odd, as Duncan said to me, not least because Everton had so recently allowed their manager to splash out the best part of £500,000 on himself and Rioch. In McKenzie's book, that hardly seemed to signal the imminent exit of Billy Bingham. But Duncan heard the news of the sacking on the radio 'and I immediately wondered whether I would be following shortly. I fervently hoped not; but you never could tell.' Johnny Carey, the man sacked by John Moores during a taxi ride, had lost his job at

Nottingham Forest only months after McKenzie had signed professional for them; Clough had made his exit from Leeds; now Bingham was on his way. 'It seemed I'd done the hat-trick, and it made me wonder if I really was a jinx, so far as managers were concerned,' Duncan said to me with a wry smile.

He wondered, of course, who would move in as Bingham's successor and if the new boss would fancy his style of play, or whether he would consider the extrovert McKenzie something of a luxury. The day after Bingham had been sacked, John Moores (he was then the vice-chairman of Everton although, clearly, he still wielded tremendous power) appeared at the Bellefield training ground. He wanted to have a chat with the players, and he told them that, for the time being, Steve Burtenshaw would take charge of team affairs – indeed, he could not be ruled out as a candidate for the job of manager. In fact, Burtenshaw acted as caretaker-manager for just a few weeks.

Meanwhile, the speculation grew and grew: Don Revie was the man who would become Everton's new manager (I was even asked to write a series of articles about Revie for the Liverpool *Daily Post* – but Revie never arrived at Goodison Park). Jimmy Armfield (the current team boss at Leeds) was about to take over at Everton; Birkenhead-born Ron Saunders, formerly an Everton player and currently enjoying success as a manager at Aston Villa, was the man for the job; Bobby Robson would be leaving Ipswich Town for Goodison Park. Last, but far from least, Everton intended to stagger the world of football by turning to the man who had guided their great rivals, Liverpool, to honours – yes, Bill Shankly.

While all this speculation was going on, Duncan McKenzie had to suffer some embarrassing moments, because of his part-time job – he and John Toshack did a radio chat-show. McKenzie was given a special assignment: to interview Billy Bingham who, perhaps surprisingly, agreed to take part. What did Bingham have to say about his sacking and his feelings? Just this: 'What I think I'll do now is become a director, and show a little bit more patience with my managers!' He did become a director, too – at Southport, for a spell, then he went back into management, with Mansfield. Once the radio interview was over, Duncan McKenzie heaved a sigh of relief and began to think about playing again. He walked into Everton's training ground one morning to discover that half a dozen reporters were waiting; and they informed him that, at last, the deed had been done. Gordon Lee was the new manager.

Under Lee, Everton went to Wembley for the 1977 League Cup final against Aston Villa, and they earned an honourable draw. Then it was on to Hillsborough for the replay – a match which, once again, ended in stalemate – and, finally, to Old Trafford for a third encounter. But that didn't turn out to be lucky for Everton, or for their manager. Brian Little's goal was the match-winner, after Everton had taken Villa right to the limit in extra time, and for Gordon Lee it was a second massive disappointment in the space of 12 months, because the previous year, as manager of Newcastle United, he had seen his side go down in the final against Manchester City.

For Duncan McKenzie, his team-mates and the Everton fans, there was another Cup drama – and another disappointment – to come. This time, against Liverpool, who had upset the odds in the Merseyside clubs' Old Trafford duel in 1971. Move on six years, and Everton were taking on Liverpool in Manchester once more, this time in the semi-final of the FA Cup, and the venue was Maine Road, where the fans saw a thriller and Everton finished up with the feeling that they had been robbed. According to McKenzie, as he told it to me: 'There isn't an Evertonian living who doesn't believe it should have been Everton going to Wembley to meet Manchester United in the final. That Saturday afternoon, we beat Liverpool all ends up – we even scored a goal which, I am convinced, was a good winner.' But that 'goal' didn't count, because it was ruled out by the referee, Clive Thomas.

It was Liverpool who scored first, McKenzie who struck an equaliser; then Liverpool scored again, and Rioch made it 2–2. By that stage, Everton were in command, although as the minutes ticked away the players and fans were all beginning to think in terms of a replay. Then Everton broke forward, and the ball was crossed from the left for McKenzie to nod it on. And this was where all the arguments began. According to Duncan, 'Bryan Hamilton took the ball on his thigh and steered it past Ray Clemence and into the net. Some folk thought Clive Thomas had disallowed the goal because he thought Bryan had handled; others believed it was an offside decision against Hammy, although the linesman's flag was never raised.'

The referee simply said afterwards that there had been 'an infringement', and he remained adamant about his decision. So Maine Road staged a replay, a match in which Liverpool cruised to victory and on to Wembley. As McKenzie told me, 'We were simply not in the right mood, after our bitter disappointment of the previous Saturday. Somehow, we just couldn't get going. Even in the dressing-room beforehand, I sensed that we were like players who had been beaten, and not played the opposition off the park a few days previously.' Since I watched that replay, I could well understand what McKenzie meant – from the moment Everton conceded a penalty (they claimed it was dubious, but Phil Neal stuck the spot-kick away), it seemed there could be only one winner. Two more goals went into Everton's net during the second half, and Liverpool were on their way to Wembley. If it hadn't been Everton's day on the Saturday, it most certainly wasn't their night when they met Liverpool the second time around.

Well, time moves on, and so do players and managers. Duncan McKenzie joined Chelsea, then Blackburn Rovers;

Gordon Lee made his exit from Goodison Park, and in came Howard Kendall who suffered his own trials and tribulations before he emerged as a hero when he steered Everton to honours at home and in Europe during their most successful period in modern times. Colin Harvey's reign came to an end on a sad note, then Kendall returned to try to work some more magic. He achieved partial success, notably after that 4–4 FA Cup draw which preceded the resignation of Kenny Dalglish at Liverpool (Everton won the replay 1–0).

There was also a success in another derby game, after Kendall had signed Peter Beardsley from Liverpool during the Graeme Souness era at Anfield. The sale of Beardsley, at £1.5 million, was controversial enough so far as the Liverpool faithful were concerned. Then the little Geordie made it a nightmare for Souness and his team as he struck the goal which ensured an Everton victory over Liverpool at Goodison Park. It was 1–1, and there were no more than half a dozen minutes left on the clock when Beardsley got possession and put the ball beyond the reach of keeper Mike Hooper. Another Anfield old boy, Gary Ablett (who, like Beardsley, had played in that 4–4 epic) helped to set up the winner for Everton at Goodison. It was only Everton's second home League victory of the season, and their first over Liverpool since they had ended the Reds' record-equalling unbeaten run in 1988. Beardsley expressed the hope that 'this will give us a big lift. We have been struggling at home, but this could set us up for the rest of the season.' He wasn't to know it then, but before long he would be on his travels again – back to Newcastle United, as Everton recouped their outlay. As for Howard Kendall, his days were also numbered and he left Goodison Park for a second time, sad that he had not been able to turn things round as he would have wished. In breezed Mike Walker, and after he had had a go at putting things right, the door was opened, at long last, for Everton old-boy Joe Royle.

Chapter Seven

TROUBLES IN TRIPLICATE

They say that troubles never come singly and that things always happen in threes. Everton certainly had managerial problems in triplicate during the 1990s as Colin Harvey, Howard Kendall and Mike Walker made their exit as team bosses at Goodison Park. Two of this trio had been players with the club and, indeed, enjoyed successful careers while wearing the royal-blue jersey. Walker was the newcomer from outside. In the case of Howard Kendall, he was moving out for the second time, after an initial spell in the hot seat which, ultimately, had brought the Goodison club almost unqualified success and, indeed, made Everton's manager a hero all over again, after the high regard in which he had been held while still a player.

Not that Kendall's managerial path had been strewn with roses all the way, during his first stint at Goodison. In fact, he had had to endure some bitter moments and suffer some biting criticism as results failed to match up to the expectations of the fans. It got to the stage, indeed, where there were more than mutterings in the media about Howard Kendall's job being on the line. Not only that, the fans had begun to turn on the manager, with slogans being painted on the walls of his garage at home and leaflets being distributed outside the ground. Then, in remarkable fashion, Kendall had gone on to bring honours to the Goodison Park club in a manner which had never been achieved by any of his predecessors.

It was generally accepted that one result in particular turned the tide in Kendall's favour. This was in 1984, when Everton travelled to the Manor Ground to meet Oxford United in a Milk Cup-tie. Defeat seemed to be staring Kendall's side in the face, but Everton managed to earn themselves a reprieve, as Adrian Heath pounced on a back-pass by Kevin Brock – and, with that goal, the Blues from Goodison Park were able to breathe a sigh of relief. They went on from there to reach the final, which they eventually lost to Liverpool.

Yet, if the punters and the media were inclined to regard that match against Oxford as a watershed in Howard Kendall's managerial career, one former player at Everton thought – and still thinks – otherwise. For Joe Royle it was a different game which proved to be the turning point; a game which was played just before that Cup-tie. He recalled: 'Everton were playing against Coventry City, and with something like five minutes to go they were trailing by a goal. I remember that match well enough, because I'd gone to Goodison Park to see it – my interest was in an Everton player, Peter Reid, and I wanted to check on his form. I'd marked him down as a possible signing for Oldham, and he was on the bench; but when he went on as substitute, he changed the course of the game for Everton, and in those last five minutes they scored a couple of goals. Graeme Sharp hit the winner.' Sharp later cost Oldham half a million pounds, and he succeeded Joe Royle as their team boss. One former backroom man at Boundary Park told me: 'If you asked Joe, he would probably tell you that the goals Sharp scored for Oldham were a major factor in the club staying up in the top flight for a couple of seasons. Joe had a great admiration for Sharp.'

After Everton's bad luck in losing the final of the Milk Cup, they did achieve a Wembley success that same year, as they beat Watford in the FA Cup; in fact, they were to go to Wembley three years in succession and, of course, there were other triumphs along the way – two League titles and the European Cup-Winners Cup. All of which confirmed the reputation of Howard Kendall as one of English football's outstanding managers and put Everton among the top clubs in the game.

So, in 1984, it was Everton 2, Watford 0, with Graeme Sharp one of the Blues' marksmen. In 1985, it was Wembley again for Everton, although this time they were beaten by Manchester United after extra time. Norman Whiteside scored the clincher. (He was later to have a brief spell at Goodison Park, before his career was ended by injury.) In 1986, it was the first all-Merseyside FA Cup final at Wembley, with Everton finishing on the wrong end of a 3–1 scoreline, and Ian Rush – the master-marksman in derby games (he overhauled the legendary Dixie Dean's record) – striking two of the goals which sank the Blues. Once again, there was one of soccer's ironies about that, because as a youngster Rush had been an Everton supporter.

When Kendall decided that he had gone as far as he could with Everton, he set his sights on success with a Continental club, and despite the pleas of Everton fans, he took on the job of team boss at Athletic Bilbao, in Spain. On one occasion, when I talked to Howard about his success at Everton – and the turbulent times he had to endure, as well – he told me: 'I'll never forget. And one of the things it taught me is that you find out who your friends are.'

Naturally, Everton sought his advice when it came to finding a successor, and there were several names in the frame – at least, according to the media. Joe Royle, Peter Reid and Colin Harvey were all mentioned. Reid had been a Kendall signing – indeed, he once said that 'we turned the corner during my first spell at the club with the signing of terrific players like Peter Reid and Andy Gray. They were not expensive to buy, but what wonderful characters – such spirit, such ambition.' Howard also once said to me that in his book, players and managers must have ambition, otherwise they didn't match up to what he wanted. If he felt that a player lacked ambition, that was a minus and a potential reason for not signing him.

When the votes were cast, it was Colin Harvey who got the job, so he stepped up from his role as first-team coach and right-hand man to Howard Kendall. Unhappily, it turned out to have been the wrong move for him.

Harvey, who had made his Everton debut as a teenager in the cauldron that was San Siro, when they took on Inter Milan in the European Cup, had played a key role for the club as a member of the Kendall-Ball-Harvey formation. Six months passed before he made his League bow, but Everton manager Harry Catterick knew he had picked another winner. Liverpool-born and bred, Harvey (and his brother, Brian) had one ambition in life: to play football. It was Colin who got the chance to join Everton when, at the age of 16, he signed amateur forms on leaving Cardinal Grammar School. Twelve months on he became an apprentice, and the following year he was being thrown in at the deep end, in that European Cup-tie against Inter. Brian, meanwhile, tried his luck with Sheffield Wednesday and Chester, then crossed the Atlantic to play for Dallas in the newly formed North American Soccer League.

Everton's Harvey will never forget his debut; neither will he forget the first goal he ever scored for the Goodison club – it came in a derby game against Liverpool. Even so, while he was a hard-working inside-forward, he appeared to lack the necessary finishing touch, and there came a time when the Everton fans began to give him some stick. Harvey has always seemed to be a somewhat withdrawn character, and the criticism appears to have got to him during those early days in his career. Catterick knew what the lad was going through, having suffered the taunts of fans himself, and he decided to hand young Harvey the No. 6 jersey, which tended to make a player feel that he had been converted to a somewhat different role. Certainly he was allowed to feel that he was no longer expected by the fans to be a regular marksman, although he did contribute his share of goals. And his career blossomed swiftly, as he became recognised as an accomplished midfielder. He went on to collect England Under-23 honours.

There came a day when Harvey was stricken with a serious eye complaint and, for a lengthy time, it seemed as if his career was at stake; but after the shock of having lost the sight of his right eye, he fought tenaciously to keep things in perspective and, on specialist advice, he took a two-month break as he underwent treatment. It succeeded, and he returned to first-team action. Yet when he became Everton's manager, sadly for him, success did not follow.

As Joe Royle soldiered on at Oldham, Harvey was given the cash to invest heavily – Tony Cottee, for instance, arrived as a £2 million signing from West Ham, and in the course of time Harvey splashed out the best part of £1 million on midfielder Mike Milligan . . . from Oldham. Big-money signings or not – and despite the fact that Cottee kicked off with a hat-trick (against Newcastle United) and continued to score goals – Everton's fortunes went into decline. Meanwhile, Howard Kendall, having sampled the atmosphere of Bilbao, in the Basque country, was enticed back into English football by Manchester City, whose chairman at the time was Peter Swales – then, also, chairman of the England international committee.

Kendall was called upon by Swales to embark on a rescue mission, as Manchester United aspired to major honours and City floundered in their slipstream. Kendall found that he needed to win over the Manchester City faithful, and that in itself was a difficult enough job. The fans didn't take to some of his signings, for example – they felt that when he went back to Everton for players, he was making too much of a good thing. Adrian Heath, Mark Ward, Neil Pointon, they had all been at Goodison Park, although in Ward's case, he had been allowed to drift into non-League football. (Once again, by one of those strokes of soccer fate, it was Joe Royle who rescued Ward's career by signing him for £7,500 from Northwich Victoria and then turning him into a winger whose ability prompted West Ham to pay Oldham Athletic quarter of a million pounds for him.)

During Kendall's reign at Maine Road, he decided that Ward was just what was required and he tempted West Ham to do a £1 million deal – in exchange for letting Ward go to Manchester City, they could have Trevor Morley and Ian Bishop. The latter, especially, had become a firm favourite with the City supporters, and they didn't relish seeing either player leave Maine Road. Then again, when Kendall allowed left-back Andy Hinchcliffe to join Everton in a swap deal for Neil Pointon, the fans were unhappy once more. Kendall, it seemed, was looking for greater defensive solidarity than he felt Hinchcliffe provided, despite his sweet left foot and ability to get forward in style. Later still, Joe Royle was to turn Hinchcliffe into one of Everton's key players – operating wide on the left in a midfield role.

When it came to the Hinchcliffe deal, and his subsequent role under Joe Royle, this was a case (like that of Mark Ward) of another career being revived. Kendall parted with Hinchcliffe in a £1.4 million package deal which included Pointon in July 1990. But while he became more or less a first-team regular, not until Royle's arrival did he blossom as a key man. Like John Ryan during his days at Oldham (where Ryan was allowed to do what he did best – attack, and get maybe ten or more goals a season), Hinchcliffe prospered as a marksman and as a provider of goals for others with that lethal left foot of his.

During Mel Machin's spell as manager of Manchester City, the 20-year-old Hinchcliffe was reckoned to be a future England international. His boss declared: 'If I were asked to name the best left-back in the country, I would not hesitate to say Andy Hinchcliffe. He did not have enough aggression when I first came to Maine Road, but all that has changed.' Like others before him (and since), Machin came and went, and Hinchcliffe was to discover that not every team boss for whom he played felt that he was the best left-back in the country. Kendall sold him, returned to Everton to oversee him again; then Mike Walker had a turn at Goodison. But it was Joe Royle who turned the left-back into what was termed 'a born-again success', as he gave him the freedom to play wide on the left and go marauding in the opposition's half of the field. Hinchcliffe was to admit that while he had always enjoyed his football, 'Joe Royle has boosted my confidence', while his manager declared that 'the Cup final could improve his claims for an England place. He has been around a long time, and it is a surprise to see that he is still only 26.' So the player capped at England Youth and Under-21 level found his career taking off again. Ultimately, Manchester City's loss had been Everton's gain.

Two players who did win the City fans' seal of approval were keeper Tony Coton, signed by Kendall for £1 million, and striker Niall Quinn, who generously gave City's manager full credit for having salvaged his career from the wreckage of reserve-team obscurity at Arsenal. Kendall acquired Quinn for less than £100,000, and the beanpole Irishman contrived to make and score goals to such good effect that he became an integral part of Jack Charlton's Republic of Ireland squad. Quinn suffered an injury which was to keep him out of the 1994 World Cup finals in the United States, but he made a good recovery after months on the sidelines, and by the spring of 1995 he was not only back in the international reckoning but was a target for Sporting Lisbon, who wanted to take him to Portugal for a fee close on £2 million. Indeed, a while earlier Howard Kendall had tried – and failed – to sign him for a second time.

By that time, Kendall had shaken the dust of Maine Road from his feet and returned to Everton. Before he left, however, he had been winning the fans over slowly, but surely, and then Everton beckoned. Colin Harvey, despite all his best efforts, had been dispensed with as manager. For City chairman Peter Swales it came as a shock to discover that Kendall was not only sought after by Everton, but that he wanted to return to Goodison Park. This, despite the advice of friends who said it would be a mistake for him to go back. Kendall, though, had made up his mind.

During his time at City, the England job had cropped up, and his had been one of the names touted for the hot seat. The selection committee (which consisted of Football Association chairman Sir Bert Millichip, Dick Wragg, Peter Swales, League president Bill Fox, Arthur McMullen and FA secretary Graham Kelly) sat down and pondered upon the names of likely men. Three names ultimately topped their list. These were Graham Taylor, Howard Kendall and Joe Royle. Joe, however, declined to go for an interview, and was marked down as a possible England manager at some future date. As for Kendall, he was a man caught between two stools. When he arrived at Maine Road Peter Swales said: 'I've got the best man for the job now.' And I am certain that he believed every word he spoke – at one stage during his spell as chairman, Swales told me, with a somewhat wry smile: 'I can't half pick 'em!' He was referring to the list of managers who had come and gone. When I discussed the matter later with Swales, he told me: 'Joe Royle wasn't the first choice – the man who topped the list was Graham Taylor, and he was the only one we interviewed.' Many months later, as Taylor, having landed what many people regarded as the toughest job in English football, was being pilloried by the critics while striving to steer his international team to the finals of the 1994 World Cup in the United States, Swales still persisted in pinning his faith in the former Watford and Aston Villa manager.

Swales told me: 'I still believe Graham was the best man for the job.' He also admitted that there was a fourth man who, while having failed to make the shortlist, most certainly deserved serious consideration. That man was Jack Charlton. 'There are a lot of things you can do right – with hindsight,' said Swales. Charlton was miffed because, he claimed, he never even had a reply to his application for the post of England manager. 'I can't remember why he didn't get an interview,' admitted Swales. And when I asked him why he stuck with Graham Taylor to the bitter end, he replied: 'Because I thought he could do the job. And I still think he would have done it – given a bit of luck.'

Not surprisingly, Peter Swales would have been extremely reluctant to lose Howard Kendall to the international arena, and he was very relieved when he realised that his club manager was prepared to stay at Maine Road. But then came the hammer-blow of learning that Everton wanted Howard, and that Howard wanted to go.

Kendall talked about the job at Manchester City as having been a love affair, but he compared his feelings and his ambitions for Everton as being like a marriage. Swales managed to swallow his bitter pill of disappointment and agreed to let Kendall return to Goodison Park. As he told me: 'I didn't want him to leave City; but when you know somebody wants to go, and wouldn't really be happy to stay, then there's no point in keeping him against his will. And that was the situation regarding Howard, so I didn't stand in his way.'

The return journey meant that, once again, Colin Harvey became Howard Kendall's right-hand man, but this time round the circumstances were somewhat different, in that Everton were beginning to feel the pinch after their lavish expenditure on players. Kendall did have money to spend, but there wasn't a bottomless pit. It was reported that he had gone back to City with a bid for Niall Quinn – and been snubbed; he did manage to sign one or two players – Mo Johnston, for instance – and did have his moments of success. Indeed, Peter Swales was one man who felt the impact of Howard Kendall's management at Everton.

It was the final day of season 1992–93, and football was buzzing with rumours and stories. Graeme Souness was going to get the chop at Liverpool (instead, he gained a reprieve); Oldham Athletic, after having looked doomed to relegation from the Premier League, saved their bacon with a dramatic 4–3 victory over Southampton; and Everton went to Maine Road and inflicted a humiliating 5–2 defeat upon Manchester City. (Oddly enough, Kendall's successor at City had been Peter Reid, whom he had signed for a second time and who had done him proud. When Kendall left, Reid took over as player-manager.)

On the last day of the season, the fans turned on Peter Swales after Everton's nap hand of goals (Swales didn't endear himself to the supporters later, when he sacked Reid, who had been a popular figure) and at the final whistle, the City chairman needed a bodyguard of burly stewards. But even so, he was hit by an egg as the fans pelted missiles in the direction of the box. Howard Kendall, sitting in front of Swales in the Maine Road stand, was also hit by an egg. Swales said: 'I don't mind the booing – I can take that; but I don't like things being thrown. It was a bad result, and I feel desperately sorry for the supporters. I understand their feelings.' And so, with the City fans chanting 'Swales out! Swales out!', Howard Kendall and his team made their exit from Maine Road. Not long afterwards, Swales himself was leaving, as former player Francis Lee finally succeeded in his takeover bid.

In the meantime, Howard Kendall was left to do battle with doughty opponents such as Kenny Dalglish, and it was a Liverpool-Everton derby game of high drama which produced yet another sensational match. The Merseyside clubs were paired with each other in the fifth round of the FA Cup, and the game in question went on at Goodison Park. It ended in a 4–4 draw – and not many hours later, Kenny Dalglish had quit his job at Anfield. The teams had drawn in the first encounter, at Anfield, the previous Sunday; this time, as the goals flowed, it became what Kendall termed 'one of the greatest Cup-ties Merseyside – if not football – has ever seen'. Four times Liverpool forged ahead, and four times Everton clawed back the goals, with Tony Cottee striking after 89 minutes to take the match into extra time. Along the way, Ian Rush scored his 24th goal in derby games against Everton and took his FA Cup tally to 37 – leaving him just four goals short of Denis Law's all-time record.

Peter Beardsley, later to be sold by Graeme Souness to Everton, put Liverpool ahead in the 33rd minute; Cottee planted the ball between the legs of Bruce Grobbelaar in the 114th minute; and in between there were half a dozen other goals for the fans to savour. Cottee, a two-goal hero, had gone on as a second-half substitute for the leg-weary Pat Nevin. He admitted that during the previous months, 'I've had my highs and my lows – that sums up my season. But it was fantastic for our fans.' Liverpool defender Gary Ablett (another player sold by Souness to Everton) said: 'I haven't played in a game like that since I was at school. When you score four goals away from home, you expect to win, but we were sloppy at the back and got punished for it. We were told about it in the dressing-room afterwards.'

Ian Rush admitted that 'you have to give Everton credit', while Graeme Sharp – an Everton marksman – declared it to have been 'the greatest game I've ever played in. I'm looking forward to the next one, but I'll have to give my legs a rest first. I'm worn out.' Sharp was to give his legs a lot more running about as he played a part in Oldham Athletic's bid to stay in top-flight football.

By the time the second replay took place (Everton won it, 1–0), Dalglish had gone and Ronnie Moran was in temporary charge at Liverpool. Howard Kendall admitted that he was staggered when he learned about Kenny's departure. 'I didn't notice anything strange either before or after the game,' he said. 'Like everybody else, I was shocked when he left – but

I understood the reasons for him leaving. There are times when you feel you've done enough.' Such a time arrived for Kendall himself, after his strenuous efforts to turn things round at Goodison Park during his second spell there.

His departure came hard on the heels of a single-goal victory over Southampton – a goal scored by Tony Cottee, whose Everton future had been clouded with controversy, and who eventually returned to his first love, West Ham. It was Everton's first home victory in the Premiership since they had beaten Liverpool in mid-September – and the attendance figures said a great deal, for the crowd of 13,660 represented Goodison Park's lowest gate of the season for a League match.

I have known Howard Kendall for a very long time. Years ago, when he was manager of Blackburn Rovers (then a struggling club), I edited their programme and wrote Howard's notes, just as I used to compile the programme notes for Kenny Dalglish when he was the team boss at Liverpool. Once upon a time the pair were rivals on Merseyside, but their fortunes have certainly contrasted in recent seasons. I dare say that Howard, looking back upon his days at Blackburn, wishes he could have spent some of the money that Jack Walker provided for Kenny Dalglish. If that had happened, maybe the Championship trophy would have landed on the sideboard at Ewood Park sooner!

Come to that, Howard Kendall could probably have used Jack Walker's money to good effect during his second spell in charge at Everton. No question about one thing, though: when Kendall bowed out at Goodison Park for the second time, it hurt. The talk was that cash problems had been a major factor in his departure. There's something a touch ironic about the fact that it was Paul Rideout whose Wembley winner in 1995 paved the way to a crock of European and domestic gold for Everton, because Rideout had been a Kendall signing, at £500,000, as Everton's manager trimmed his cloth to suit his club's purse.

The parting of the ways for club and manager came after Everton had just beaten Southampton 1–0 and chairman Dr David Marsh appeared, to issue a statement. With the chairman was deputy chairman Sir Desmond Pitcher, and Marsh read the hastily written statement which had been jotted down on the back of an envelope. It said simply: 'Everton Football Club and Howard Kendall jointly announce that his position with the club has been terminated by him in accordance with the terms of his contract.' The hands on the clock that Saturday evening timed the announcement at 5.34. Kendall had been at Goodison Park for three years, but success the second time around had eluded him, even though, after three games that season, Everton had led the way at the top of the table. But that position had flattered them, as the later part of the season demonstrated.

The end came with startling suddenness; few people had been in on the secret. Tony Cottee, Everton's match-winner, was taken by surprise, as were his team-mates. As he drove home from the match, listening to the car radio, the news came through. 'I thought that if he was going to quit, he might have gone after the United match. He stayed and seemed quite happy,' said Cottee. 'The United match' had taken place in midweek, when Everton had gone down and out of the Coca-Cola Cup against Manchester United. Afterwards, Everton's manager admitted: 'My current spell at Everton has proved the most frustrating period of my entire career. [He was to suffer even more later, when he was sacked by Notts County in bizarre fashion after a mere ten-week spell at the helm.] It would hurt bitterly for me to have to leave, but if it was to be in the best interests of the club, I would do it,' he said.

However, he remained in charge, and the victory over Southampton provided Everton with much-needed points and offered the prospect of better things, even though the gate had been the club's lowest in the League for ten years. Then the bombshell statement by Everton's chairman.

Kendall himself had already said his piece to the media. Shortly after the final whistle he climbed the stairs and entered the press room to talk about the game. No hint of what was to follow.

Usually, someone starts the ball rolling and then the questions and observations come thick and fast. The match had been nothing to write home about, however, and this time there was an air of disinterest, with few questions being thrown at the manager. Howard Kendall has always been articulate, but on this occasion everyone appeared to be stuck for words, and there were some lengthy silences. Kendall observed: 'I take it you have not been too excited, gentlemen, today. I am all right tonight. All right. Okay.' And that was just about it, as Howard Kendall made his exit, and left the way clear for Ian Branfoot, who was then the manager of Southampton. Like Kendall, he knows what it's like to become the victim of a hate campaign by the fans, and in the end he parted company with Southampton. Indeed, only a week previously Branfoot had admitted: 'It has reached the stage where I wonder if I am being followed home in my car. I believe that it is just an extension of the violent society we now live in.' Now, in Everton's press room and in the wake of defeat, he spoke of his disappointment at the result. 'I felt if we could have knocked one in we would probably have won the game, because the crowd would have turned on them.' (In fact, the fans hadn't turned on Howard Kendall in the way they did ten years earlier – this time, it was recorded, 'they have voted with their feet'. Ten years previously, Everton's chairman at the time, Philip Carter, had kept his nerve and given Howard Kendall a vote of confidence in the face of the fans' fury; it was a vote of confidence which Kendall repaid, because between 1984 and 1987 Everton collected one trophy after another, to claim more silverware than at any other time in the club's history.)

With Kendall's departure, the name of Peter Reid cropped up as a possible successor, along with that of Joe Royle, not to mention Steve Coppell and Ron Atkinson. Reid, signed by Kendall both for Everton and for Manchester City, had lost his job as team boss at Maine Road shortly after a defeat at Goodison Park in the first week of the season. Then he had gone back, to playing, for Southampton. However, the 37-year-old Reid had not been in Southampton's side at Goodison; injury had kept him on the sidelines. It was reported that 'Whether it is Reid, Coppell, Royle, Bruce Rioch or anyone else, he will face the same catch-22 situation as Kendall, unless showbusiness impresario Bill Kenwright, likely to take over as chairman, with the support of the controlling Moores family, can raise millions to fund big signings.' That didn't happen, because Peter Johnson became the top man at Goodison, although cash then was found to bring in expensive, big-name players.

In the meantime, and having slept upon matters, Howard Kendall accepted his share of the blame as he said: 'This is a desperately disappointing situation in which I have not done what was wanted by the people that I love – and that hurts.' After the millions of pounds which had been spent by Colin Harvey, Kendall had invested more, especially £1.5 million on Mo Johnston – a move which had not been repaid with results.

'I would like to think that right to the final whistle I did my job professionally. With the players not knowing the situation, it proved that I did that, and the club got the three points which were much needed.' Having decided that enough was enough, Howard also said: 'As far as I am concerned, it will always be a case of separation, never divorce. I'll bounce back. I'll be looking for another job as quickly as possible.' In fact, he had a brief spell as manager of a Greek club, then embarked upon his ill-fated mission to save Notts County from relegation. As for the club which had been his first love, it was said that 'for both Everton and Howard Kendall, it will never be quite the same again'.

The midweek defeat by Manchester United had clearly

given Kendall food for thought – especially thought about whether or not the Everton supporters were beginning to lose faith in him. Then came the story about his failure to persuade the board to back a £1.5 million bid to land Dion Dublin from Old Trafford. And, finally, the knowledge that the gate for the game against Southampton was the lowest in a decade. Kendall walked away from Goodison Park, and while the guessing game about Everton's new manager gathered pace, so did the speculation about the identity of the club's new chairman, with former *Coronation Street* actor Bill Kenwright being tipped to succeed Dr David Marsh.

While Kendall refused to offer any comment on the Dion Dublin affair, Dr Marsh, while declining to mention individual players, did say: 'I don't think these sort of things are rows. If there is discussion about any player, you sit long and hard and talk about it. If you have a load of cash you don't talk about it enough; if you are short of cash, you talk about it even harder. There are no rows, just different opinions.' The chairman admitted that 'we had an inkling of something towards the end of the match against Southampton, and Howard told us officially afterwards'. After having gone to Everton's Bellefield training ground to collect his things, Kendall declared; 'I have absolutely no doubt I have made the right decision. It had to be done, and you don't make a decision like this and regret it 24 hours later.' He stressed that speculation about future control of the Goodison Park club had had nothing to do with his decision to quit.

The speculation took several twists and turns before Everton and their supporters knew the outcome. Along with Bill Kenwright, the name of Peter Johnson began to come into the reckoning – and he, it was reported, had been (indeed, he still might well be) a Liverpool fan. On the managerial front, there was more gossip. While Howard Kendall's name was being linked with both the England vacancy and the job which was going at Sunderland, it was reported that Peter Reid had been 'installed as favourite' for Goodison Park, while 'Rioch, Royle and Coppell also have support'. Everton, in fact, did have something of a history for keeping the managerial job 'in the family' – Harry Catterick, Howard Kendall, Colin Harvey had all played for the club, as had Rioch and Royle. 'But within the club, and among many fans,' it was said, 'there is a feeling that a character like Ron Atkinson is needed to inspire the revival.'

Chairman Marsh played it cool. 'We will wait and see what comes along. We will invite applications. There is no time limit, but you don't want a rudderless ship. If someone comes along with the right credentials, he will be considered.' Reserve-team coach Jimmy Gabriel – another former Everton player – took over for the next match, away against Manchester City, and he had been in charge for one game after the sacking of Colin Harvey. That match had been against Queen's Park Rangers, and Everton had won it, 3–0. But as had happened in 1990, Gabriel didn't get the job on a permanent basis.

Ron Atkinson did seem to have the right credentials; he had managed Manchester United with considerable success, his teams had always played with the kind of flair the Everton fans appreciated, and he was a Liverpudlian by birth. He had been the rounds, from struggling clubs to wealthy ones, and he knew what was what. But when the decision was made, it wasn't Atkinson's name in the frame. Norwich City manager Mike Walker was the man upon whom the choice fell. Not that it proved an easy matter to prise Walker away from Carrow Road – or, rather, Norwich City were the ones who proved difficult to deal with. But, in the end, Everton got their man, as well as a new supremo in the shape of Peter Johnson. What was to follow turned out to be a testing time.

Chapter Eight

THE GREAT ESCAPE

Football has its firebrands and its rogues, its jokers and its clowns, its born-again Christians and its characters who steer so close to the wind that they sometimes risk the threat of going to jail. Glamour? That's when you walk up the steps to the royal box to collect your FA Cup-winner's medal, or when you're holding aloft a European trophy. It's at such times that you and your team-mates are the darlings of the fans; you can do no wrong, even if that is merely a temporary state of affairs. Talk to a footballer's wife, and you may well see things through different eyes as another kind of picture comes into the frame.

Talk to Janet Royle, for instance, and listen to her story of having been a footballer's wife for 25 years. Jan Royle is married to someone who has known the bad times as well as the good during his career as a manager. When Janet Hughes met Joe Royle when they were both 17, she didn't take any interest in football and she had no idea that her husband-to-be was an up-and-coming starlet with Everton. She had a brother called Harry who was 15 and a Liverpool supporter. That, of course, changed; young Harry became an Everton fan. By the same token, when Joe Royle was handed the job of managing Everton, after a dozen years at Oldham Athletic, I asked Jan how she and the rest of the family felt about it – after all, Joe had become the League's longest-serving manager, once Brian Clough had hung up that old green jersey, and he appeared to have a job for life at Oldham. 'I'm pleased for Joe – though it's a wrench for him to leave Oldham. In fact, Mark [their youngest son] is very upset about it – he's been brought up here and he's an Oldham fan through and through.' No doubt the appearance of Everton in the 1995 FA Cup final helped young Mark to come to terms with his dad's switch of allegiance.

Janet Royle discovered among other things that football can be a career which makes nomads of those closely involved in the game. Even back in the early days she got an inkling of what it would be like – and an indication of the inherent dangers which lurked every time Joe went out to play for Everton. She can recall one occasion when he was playing for the reserves, and the opposition's goalkeeper and another player fell in a heap with Joe underneath the pair of them. Joe finally emerged, picked himself up and dusted himself down, then got on with the game; but not for long. He had bruised his ribs badly in that mêlée, and he had to go off and retire to bed.

Jan Royle used to sit and watch Joe in action, and all the time she was willing him to do well and to avoid injury. Sometimes she would sit there, screwing her handkerchief into a little ball as her eyes followed Joe's every move down on the pitch. 'I used to worry about him being injured,' she told me, adding: 'Now that he's a manager, I worry about results. Though the first couple of years were the worst.' Then, Joe was almost trying to make bricks without straw at Boundary Park. And, of course, he was still striving to prove that he could make a good manager. 'In the beginning, it was very hard for him,' Jan said. And for her, as well.

During Joe Royle's early days as a player at Everton, he and his girlfriend would go out for a meal and, as often as not, they would try to pick a place where they could eat in peace. It wasn't all glamour, having a boyfriend who was in the public eye, especially when there were Liverpool fans all ready to have a little joke and dispense a few merry quips about someone who wore the wrong team colours. So the couple would often find a place out of town. If they did go in a group to a club, they would find themselves splitting up, because while Jan liked to dance Joe preferred to have a little flutter. He wasn't especially keen on dancing, even though he could be light on his feet when it came to football.

Jan worried, too, when there were reports that Everton were likely to pay £100,000 for Rangers striker Colin Stein midway through season 1968-69, because that could mean Joe having to look elsewhere for a first-team spot. It didn't happen, but it did demonstrate the uncertainty of a footballer's life; one day you're a star, the next you're on your bike to another club. In Joe's case, when the move did come, it was to another club whose players wore blue shirts – Manchester City – so there were no problems about moving miles away from Merseyside. But that situation changed as the years came and went.

Jan told me how, in their courting days, they decided to get married when they were both 21 – until their plans hit a snag. By that time, the 1970 World Cup was coming up in Mexico, and the talk was that Joe Royle might well figure in Ramsey's plans. Indeed, one sports columnist had written: 'Royle, established among the fast-maturing young stars at Everton, is a solid bet to advance from Under-23 level to win a place in England's World Cup squad for Mexico in 1970. He is over six foot, yet has the balance and poise of a featherweight. It may not be long before Royle is accepted in the same ranking as the other crack centre-forwards who have starred for Everton, Dixie Dean and Tommy Lawton.' Jan Royle recalled that she had agreed, if need be, to postpone the wedding plans. 'Yes, we did change the date – Joe was placed on standby, but he wasn't called up.'

Just another of those little things sent to try the wife of a professional footballer. And, of course, now and again a footballer's girlfriend or wife – come to that, a manager's wife, too – has to sit and listen to fans who are not fussy in their language when it comes to describing, out loud, the failings of someone whom they consider to have let them down. In Joe Royle's case, there came a time when he was a genuine candidate for the England job, and when I talked to him about that, he told me, with engaging candour: 'Yes, I was invited to go for an interview but, to be honest, I didn't think it was worth going for the job. For one thing, I didn't feel as if I was ready for it. I was still a Second Division manager who hadn't won anything. And, for another thing, I wasn't ready to give up the day-to-day involvement which being manager of a League club brings.' So Graham Taylor really had no competition, what with Howard Kendall backing off as well.

Joe's move to Manchester City saw him going to Wembley with his second club, this time for the final of the Football League Cup. Capped 14 times at England Under-23 level and half a dozen times as a senior international, he had packed a lot of experience, as well as 100 goals, into his career, and in season 1975-76 the Wembley duel between Manchester City and Newcastle United ended up 2–1 in City's favour. Newcastle's team boss was Gordon Lee, the man who, 12 months on, was to steer Everton to Wembley in the League Cup and wind up on the losing end yet again. When Joe Royle went to Wembley with City, it was a spectacular overhead kick from Dennis Tueart which won the match for the men from Maine Road, with Peter Barnes City's other marksman. Joe Royle, of course, played up front, and in defence was a Scotland international who later became his right-hand man at both Oldham and Everton – Willie Donachie. One Thursday afternoon, in the spring of 1995, I met Willie and his wife, Yvonne, in the carpark of our local Sainsbury's. When I asked Willie what he was doing there, he smiled and answered: 'I'm taking a few hours off – we've got a reserve game tonight, so I'm going back to Goodison.' Yvonne told me: 'I've only seen him for a few hours since he went to Everton six months ago – at least, that's what it seems like!' I knew just what she meant, because once the game gets into your blood, football comes first, last and always.

Many years ago, there was a Glenn Miller film called *Orchestra Wives* which related how the wives of itinerant musicians had to follow the band and sit and watch the groupies make a play for the big-name instrumentalists. No one would dispute that there are groupies in football, too – they follow the stars around and, often as not, are prepared to put temptation in their way. Joe Royle and Willie Donachie have always had their heads screwed on, and they're both home birds, though they can enjoy a drink and a laugh with anyone. Joe and Jan started married life in a two-bedroom detached house on Merseyside. 'We loved it there,' said Jan. After the move to Manchester, they lived in a newly built house at Ormskirk, near Southport, and then it was a long-distance job, as Joe's career took him to Bristol and Norwich.

In East Anglia, where the countryside is as flat as a pancake, they bought a house – and later, after the move to Oldham, they found that they couldn't sell it, for a long time; in Bristol, they rented a detached house, then bought and renovated an old house which had been built at the beginning of the century. 'It was really two big cottages which had been knocked into one in an acre of land. We had a herb garden, and fruit and vegetables – Joe did a lot of the work himself. He prefers the country lifestyle.' It was Bristol-Norwich-Oldham, and when the house in East Anglia 'stuck', Joe and Jan rented a modern house for a spell. It was at a place called Dunham Massey, just inside the Cheshire boundary, and the owner was former England star Trevor Francis, who lived in the house next door. Finally, the Royles moved out and into their own place, high on the moors above Oldham, on the border of a village called Saddleworth.

Home then was what Jan called 'an ex-sanatorium' – once

upon a time it had housed people who suffered from tuberculosis. 'The building really was a shell – the walls were standing, but there was no roof, and there were holes where the windows had been. We bought it as a derelict place and then we had it done up. By the time we had it as we wanted, there were five bedrooms, three bathrooms, a room for the kids, and one-third of an acre of land. We had a rugged garden with a rockery round it, and Joe built a fish pond. It suited our needs more than any house we had had; despite its size, we use every inch of it.'

Naturally, Joe's move to Everton prompted the question: 'Does this mean you'll be on your travels again?' It brought the cautious answer from Joe Royle: 'We'll just have to wait and see how things go.' Like many other football nomads, he was prepared to see how he got on, driving the best part of 50 miles each way every working day before he uprooted again. As Janet Royle said: 'We have loved it here, and we've put a lot into the house. We've grown attached to the old place, after a dozen years. Joe loves to potter in the garden when he gets the time and our three sons have more or less been brought up here.' And yes, they would all like to be footballers, 'but you have to have a special talent for that'. In fact, the eldest son, Lee, now in his mid-20s, became a sales executive for a builders merchants, while Darren, having got three A-levels, was going on to college. And young Mark was still at school.

If Oldham's loss was Everton's gain, at least the Boundary Park club could look back on some exciting times during the Joe Royle era. Oldham had raised a few eyebrows when they parted company with that quietly spoken Scot, Jimmy Frizzell, who had served them long and well both as player and manager. He landed a job at Manchester City, while Joe Royle, to the surprise of some people, was handed the task of trying to take Latics into a higher grade of football. It turned out to be a job and a half, with no little heartache, not to mention anxiety in the early years. Even when the club was achieving success, Oldham's manager wondered whether or not enough fans cared enough to give the club the necessary support – and, like the fans everywhere, there were times when the supporters turned somewhat fickle. But through it all, Royle and Oldham made steady progress.

When Kevin Keegan went into management and proved so successful, his former Liverpool team-mate, John Toshack, admitted that he 'didn't think he had it in him'. To be honest, neither did I; and, for that matter, I wondered if Joe Royle would turn out to be one of those who had enjoyed success as a player but who would find the going much tougher as a manager. It had happened to other illustrious names before him such as Stanley Matthews and Bobby Charlton, to mention but two.

Gradually, though, Oldham Athletic developed a style of play which had their fans on the edge of their seats – and sometimes with their hearts in their mouths. The same applied to their manager, who had moulded an entertaining, attacking side which, on its day, could rattle in the goals – and, on its off-day, concede them in similar fashion. Go to a match at Boundary Park and you could expect to be entertained; you could also expect anything to happen, right to the final whistle, even if Oldham were winning 4-1 with quarter of an hour to go.

I can remember a bitterly cold night when the snow was falling and Oldham hammered Ipswich Town, who were going for promotion. Ipswich had stayed overnight at a first-class hotel, and they had every incentive to go out and give a good account of themselves; yet, on the night, it was Oldham who played with pride and passion, and they pasted Ipswich. Just like they gave Arsenal a beating in a Cup-tie which led to their manager, George Graham, admitting that this was a result which was 'unacceptable' for a club of Arsenal's standing – although, having said that, all credit to Oldham.

When Oldham were playing in Cup-ties, they showed

that they could go to grounds like Goodison Park and The Dell and get a result. Former Everton player Ian Marshall earned his side a replay, and Everton suffered at Boundary Park. Oldham snatched a last-minute equaliser at Southampton, and the Saints were snuffed out at Boundary Park. On a midweek night, West Ham went out to contest the semi-final, first leg of the Littlewoods Cup – and they scarcely knew what had hit them, as the Latics hammered six goals past the Hammers' keeper. The return match, of course, appeared to be a formality, and so it should have been; but – Oldham being Oldham – they found themselves three goals down with something like half the game still to play. They managed to weather the Upton Park storm, and so they went to Wembley, where Nottingham Forest conquered them by the only goal of the game.

I can remember Oldham, fighting to preserve their top-flight status, taking on Manchester United and beating them with a Neil Adams goal – he's not the tallest player in the game, but he had got up to nod the ball past the giant Dane, Peter Schmeichel. In another encounter with Alex Ferguson's team, Oldham gave their all – yet still conceded half a dozen goals as Manchester United turned on the style. Oldham and Leeds had some rare tussles, and when the Latics met Sheffield Wednesday the rivalry was spiced by the fact that the respective managers, Joe Royle and Ron Atkinson, were close friends off the field.

The season that Oldham arrived in the First Division was one for their fans to recall, not least because the final match was against Sheffield Wednesday, and the result could determine which of the clubs finished as champions of the Second Division. Ron Atkinson was not a happy man, as he saw his team beaten at the last gasp, so that Wednesday finished in third place (they still went up) while the Latics emerged as top dogs. That was one of the high spots of Joe Royle's career at Boundary Park, and another was the week when Oldham staged a Houdini act to preserve their Premier

League status. Once again, Ron Atkinson (by this time managing Aston Villa and aiming to steer them to the Championship, as they fought it out with Manchester United) was made to suffer agonies. Oldham travelled to Villa Park to try their luck on the Sunday afternoon and everyone regarded this one as a formality for Villa. At that stage, with three games to go, Oldham looked to be dead and buried – but they scored the only goal, to give themselves a brief glimpse of hope. The next test was in midweek, against Liverpool, however, and once again few gave the Latics a chance, even though the side managed by Graeme Souness had been having problems.

That same night, Crystal Palace played at Maine Road, and their 0-0 draw against Manchester City appeared to edge them closer to salvation, as they totalled 49 points for the season. However, Oldham came good once more, as they subjected Liverpool to a 3-2 defeat which, it was recorded, 'piled shame upon a club which, not long ago, stood for everything good in football'. It was said that 'Oldham and their fans danced with delight at the final whistle, their first victory over Liverpool in 71 years offering hope of Premier League survival'. And so Oldham reached the final day of the campaign knowing that after having sprung two shock results, they might still be saved. Although it would require them to do something they had so far failed to achieve all season – and that was to win three matches in succession. Further, of course, they must still rely upon Crystal Palace being beaten by Arsenal at Highbury.

It turned out to be an astonishing finale to the season, in several different ways. I have seen some soccer cliffhangers in my time; at World Cup level, in Europe, and on the domestic front; and the Oldham Athletic-Southampton match compares with the best of them. I was there to witness the drama for myself, and it still remains vivid in my mind. It was what one of the Sunday papers next morning termed 'the Great Escape', and the story beneath this headline began: 'Jubilant Joe Royle dispensed with humility over shoestring Oldham's miraculous survival to stay among the élite. "We deserve to be in the Premier League, and they should be delighted to have us," said the Oldham manager, after another enthralling, nail-biting day at Boundary Park.'

After the heart-stopper against Southampton, it was recorded that Oldham's third victory in a row had kept them in the top flight, and ahead of Crystal Palace, on mere goal difference; and Royle was quoted thus: 'They call Old Trafford the Theatre of Dreams but, for sheer excitement, this is the place to be. We won't win the Premier League next season [in fact, Oldham suffered relegation], but there must be a place for a team like us. There has got to be some romance in the game, as well as money and power, and we provide it.' Little did he know, then, that before long he would be 'shopping at Harrods' with the new-found wealth of Everton.

At the time of 'the Great Escape', though, he remembered the manager whose side had failed to survive in the top echelon of English football – the result at Highbury [Arsenal 3, Crystal Palace 0] had left Steve Coppell shell-shocked and miserable. It was one of those ironies of football that Joe Royle and Steve Coppell had been schoolmates at Quarry Bank High and at Ranworth Square, so it was with genuine feeling that Joe declared: 'I feel sorry for Steve, who is a close friend. It's tough on Palace to go down with 49 points, but our saving grace is that we score goals – that's what has kept us up.' Coppell, meanwhile, was saying his piece; 'I'm as guilty as anybody.' And he cast doubts about his own position as he added: 'I haven't got many options, have I? I'm still in contract, but where relegation is involved, you can't blame other people. I feel the blow personally, and I am as guilty as anyone. I steered a ship . . . it ran aground. We were afraid to make mistakes today and put in a limited display.' He did say, too: 'If I wished anybody to stay up in our place, I'm pleased it is my pal Joe Royle. Oldham have put in a superhuman effort recently, but it seemed over the last week that fate would conspire against us when they won at Villa Park.'

Southampton were under constant pressure, as Oldham drove forward in numbers, and they managed to hold out for the first half-hour. Then a corner kick from left-back Neil Pointon went past keeper Tim Flowers, and the home fans rejoiced. They celebrated yet again, despite the fact that Matthew Le Tissier struck an equaliser after 35 minutes, because with 60 seconds to go to half-time, Andy Ritchie set up a scoring chance for Royle's £750,000 signing, Ian Olney, and he made no mistake. Next came a stunning header from Ritchie himself, and then it was the turn of Norwegian international Gunnar Halle to score, so with 25 minutes to go and Oldham leading by four goals to one, it seemed all that was required was for Arsenal to stay in front of Crystal Palace at Highbury.

That was never in doubt; but up at Boundary Park Le Tissier and his team-mates hadn't given up the ghost. As their manager, Ian Branfoot, said afterwards: 'I was pleased about the way they reacted – they showed they weren't ready just to roll over and die.' And they didn't. Once again, Le Tissier did the damage, and the scoreline swiftly altered from 4–1 to 4–2 and then to 4–3. Suddenly, with five minutes still to go, it became apparent to the thousands who had been roaring Latics on to victory and Premier League survival that their team was not out of the woods yet. However, to the distinct relief of the home supporters, Oldham managed to cling on to their slender lead, and when the final whistle went Joe Royle and his backroom men leaped off their seats in the dug-out and raised their arms in the air. Royle declared: 'It's been an amazing day – another one of those games that puts five years on me. But I must say that we have never given up hope, and I'm delighted for everyone.'

Joe smiled wryly, as he also said: 'We play the game with

the right attitude – but I sometimes think that my team is trying to kill me! My nerves are shredded. At the end, I went on the pitch to ask the referee jokingly if he had a proper watch, because he had played so much injury time.' Players and manager took their bow as they did a lap of honour in celebration of their great escape, then finally they retreated to the haven of the dressing-room. I was able to get down there and I have to say that, on walking inside, the scene that met me was somewhat surprising. I had expected to see the players almost delirious with delight, shouting and joking and generally celebrating, but they sat there on the benches around the dressing-room, draped in towels as well as covered in sweat after their exertions; and they didn't exactly seem like a bunch of lads who had just escaped the guillotine. Most of them, not surprisingly, looked drained – indeed, some appeared to be deathly pale and seemingly in a daze. It was as if they still hadn't been able to take in the fact that it was all over and the miracle had happened. But, of course, as the clock ticked on and the realisation sank home, it was time to uncork the champagne and celebrate.

Just one year on, however, and the scene was totally different as Oldham Athletic, despite their gallant efforts, finally sank through the relegation trapdoor. And not so many months later, their manager and his second-in-command were on their way to Goodison Park, there to embark upon yet another, desperate salvage operation.

Chapter Nine

THE MIDAS TOUCH

Call him the man with the Midas touch, for that's the kind of reputation which Joe Royle has acquired over the years, as he has delved into the transfer market, and the free-transfer market, and come up with players who turned out to be nuggets of pure gold. And all this in spite of the fact that, as his rival and friend, Alex Ferguson, says: 'Every signing is a gamble – even one that costs only fifty bob.'

An outstanding example of what can and does happen in football is David Platt, the kid who was released by Manchester United. He went on from Crewe Alexandra to Aston Villa, into Italian football, joined Arsenal in the summer of 1995 and thus became a player whose total transfer outlay topped £22 million! Peter Beardsley was also allowed to leave Old Trafford after a fairly brief spell during which he never even got a first-team outing at League level. He told me: 'Nothing really went wrong. It was simply that Norman Whiteside did so well that he couldn't be left out, and he went on to play for Northern Ireland in the World Cup. I knew that Vancouver Whitecaps would be happy to have me back, and so I returned to Canada.' Not for long, because Newcastle signed him for £150,000, then it was on to Liverpool, Everton and back to St James's Park, with close on £5 million changing hands altogether. Newcastle, in the summer of 1995, paid Wimbledon £4.5 million for Warren

Barton – a player who had been snapped up for £10,000, while John Scales, once a Leeds United discard, won an England cap. Scales arrived at Liverpool as a £3 million man via Bristol and Wimbledon, while Mark Ward – once an Everton reject – returned to Goodison Park as a £1 million signing by Howard Kendall for the second time around . . . after Joe Royle had plucked him from non-League football for £7,500. Ward was just one of the many bargain buys for Oldham Athletic, who transferred him to West Ham for quarter of a million and thus made a handsome profit – as happened with most of the deals Royle did on a shoestring. Some you win, and some you lose, of course. I can recall a strapping young centre-half who was wanted by half a dozen top clubs; he wound up at Everton and was thought to have a great future in the game, but before he had even got past the apprentice stage he was on his way down the divisions, and never surfaced again.

I once talked to Harry Catterick about what made a player, and what made a manager interested in signing him. Catterick said: 'I look for the player's strengths and for his weaknesses. Every player has a weakness, but it's his strength that matters to me. I try to make sure that he never makes a mistake when it comes to his strong point; then I set about trying to improve him where he's weak.'

When he managed Manchester City, Howard Kendall traded Andy Hinchcliffe for Neil Pointon, feeling that Pointon had the greater defensive qualities as a left-back. He was probably right, at that; but Joe Royle looked at things differently when he became manager of Everton. Kendall had been and gone, and Hinchcliffe had not always been first choice; neither had Paul Rideout, up front. Royle, like Catterick, assessed what each player could do best, and the result was that Hinchcliffe became a regular who was encouraged to get forward and deliver telling crosses and corners, from which Rideout and Duncan Ferguson could profit. Once Royle was at Goodison, Rideout found that he was being given his chance to partner the £4 million Scot, and he took the chance well. Royle didn't feel he had to play £3 million striker Daniel Amokachi, who had been signed during the Mike Walker era; neither did he plump for £2 million midfielder Vinny Samways. But local lad Gary Ablett, who was regarded as expendable by Graeme Souness, kept his place to become the first footballer to win an FA Cup medal with both Liverpool and Everton.

Joe Royle has long been well aware of the value of having a top-class physiotherapist on the staff, and I have always thought that a physio is, in his own sphere, just as important as the manager at a club. An aeroplane is no use when it's standing idle on the tarmac; a taxi is no use when it's standing idle in the garage; and a footballer is no use unless he's out on the pitch, performing to the best of his ability and helping to pay off a chunk of his hefty transfer fee. Yet through the years, clubs have consistently ignored the need for them to have a physio looking after the fitness of their highly paid players. Only in recent times have clubs come to terms with the wisdom of paying qualified therapists the right kind of money to tend to their soccer stars.

It was well known that Bill Shankly used to shy away when he saw one of his players on the treatment table – he didn't like the thought that the player might be missing on the Saturday afternoon. Shanks believed players should be able to shrug off minor injuries, and they often did; for one thing, they were afraid to lose their places if they cried off. There was one occasion, as Ian St John told me, laughing as he did so, when Chris Lawler, who rarely missed a match because of injury, was feeling a bit of a knock and Bob Paisley, who was in charge of the training, told Chris to do a bit of jogging on his own and make sure he didn't overdo it and make the injury worse. When Shankly arrived and saw Chris separated from the main group, and gently trotting along, he rasped out: 'What's that malingerer Lawler think he's doing!'

Bob Paisley, in fact, learned the science of physiotherapy via a correspondence course and with the help of John Moores, who arranged for him to visit local hospitals and see for himself what kind of treatment and what kind of equipment could best help people to recover full fitness. Nowadays, every club in the Premiership has to have a fully qualified physiotherapist on its staff, and that is as it should be – indeed, I believe every club in the professional game should be required to follow suit. A six-week course in the treatment of injuries is an improvement on the days when the trainer carried his 'magic sponge' on to the field when a player was injured; but it takes three years to qualify as a physio, and this includes watching operations during a spell of working in hospital, and a knowledge of how to use such aids as ultra-sound machines.

It's the job of the physio to ensure that an injured player is not rushed back into action too soon – if he is, then he's liable to aggravate the injury, and that has happened all too often, as directors and managers show their anxiety to have their best players in the team at all times. It's also the job of the physio to get injured players fully fit at the earliest possible moment – and to diagnose correctly when there is a need for the surgeon to be called in.

In football, managers have to back their judgment as well as their physios, and Joe Royle has done this in superb fashion. One bargain buy after another arrived at Boundary Park, to make good. Royle groomed full-back John Ryan, then sold him to Newcastle for £230,000. Joe Royle certainly got the best out of Ryan during his first spell at Boundary Park, because this attacking full-back could be counted upon to get into double figures for goals, season after season. In much the same way, Royle got Andy Hinchcliffe going forward and making goals after his arrival at Goodison Park. While still at Oldham, Royle invested heavily in talent from Everton: Graeme Sharp (£500,000), Neil Adams (£100,000), Neil McDonald (£500,000), Ian Marshall (£100,000), Mike

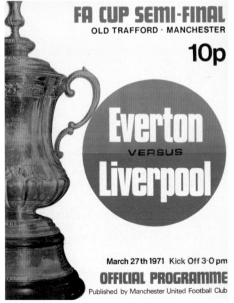

Derby game duels in the League and the FA Cup, with Everton having mixed fortunes: a 0–0 draw at Goodison Park and a 2–1 defeat at Old Trafford. But at Wembley in 1966, it was Everton 3, Sheffield Wednesday 2

On the alert: Dave Watson, Neville Southall and David Burrows guard the goalmouth

Take that! Duncan Ferguson's header beats Manchester United's Peter Schmeichel to win the Goodison encounter in 1994–95

Jumping for joy! It's two-goal hero Daniel Amokachi, whose marksmanship against Tottenham Hotspur paved the way to Wembley in 1995

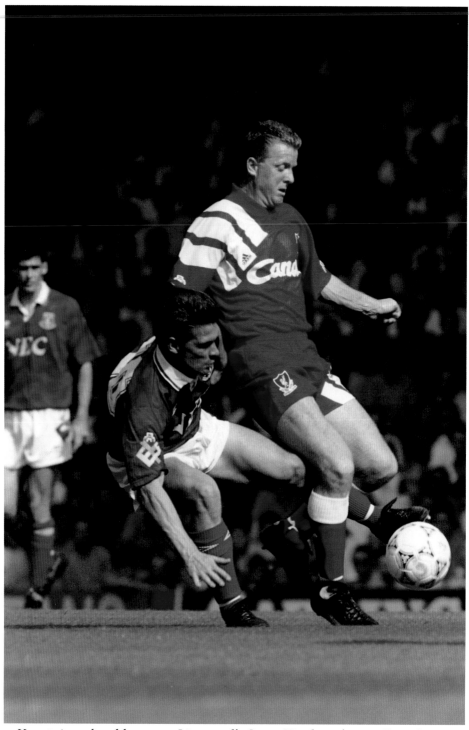

Up against the old enemy: Liverpool's Steve Nicol can't stop Tony Cottee winning the ball

No holding back! Paul Rideout tussles with John Scales of Liverpool, while Andy Hinchcliffe takes on Rob Jones

Once they were team-mates – now it's David Burrows of Everton against Liverpool's Rob Jones

No way through for Liverpool striker Robbie Fowler, as David Unsworth steers the ball away

Heading for victory: Everton at Wembley in 1995. And Paul Rideout was the match-winner against Manchester United

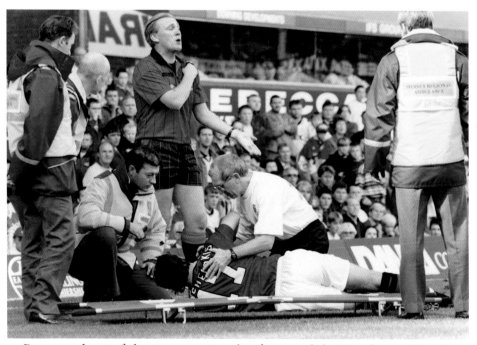

Down and out of the game against his former club, Manchester United. That's Andrei Kanchelskis, whose transfer to Everton caused controversy as it was on, off and, finally, on again

*Success! For Joe Royle and coach Willie Donachie, the 1995
victory at Wembley was something to savour*

*The FA Cup is in good hands, held aloft by Duncan Ferguson and
Paul Rideout*

Milligan (sold to Everton for almost £1 million, bought back for £600,000). In addition, he signed Mark Ward from Northwich Victoria for £7,500 after the youngster had been released by Everton, and not long before he left Oldham Royle took a player called Billy Kenny from Goodison Park. Kenny had been allowed to go after he and the club had had problems, and Joe Royle has always been ready to give a player the benefit of the doubt and take a chance on his talent. However, in Kenny's case, things didn't work out too well at Oldham either.

Go through the list of players Royle snapped up from other clubs for Oldham, and it becomes clear that he has a fancy for a player who can adapt to various roles – Marshall, at centre-half or centre-forward; Paul Warhurst, at centre-half or right-back; McDonald, at full-back or in midfield; Earl Barrett, at full-back or centre-back; Gunnar Halle, at right-back or wide on the right going forward (as Hinchcliffe does on the left for Everton); Denis Irwin, in either of the full-back positions. There were, of course, players who occupied what might be termed specialist positions – goalkeeper Andy Goram; centre-back Andy Linighan; Rick Holden, who played wide on the left; Tommy Wright, also a wide player; Andy Ritchie, a striker, as was Darren Beckford. The last-named was a fairly modest £350,000 signing from Norwich City (who had paid Port Vale £900,000 for him), although, like McDonald and Olney, Beckford discovered that his career at Oldham didn't really flourish. It becomes crystal clear, however, just how Joe Royle became the man with the Midas touch, as you go through the list of players he took from other clubs – clubs which, for one reason or another, had decided that these players didn't measure up to their own requirements. Yet in some instances players not only made good at Oldham – they made the Boundary Park club a handsome profit as they moved on to higher things themselves.

The case of full-back Denis Irwin is one of the classic

instances of snapping up a player on a free transfer and selling him on for a small fortune. Irwin had been striving to carve out a career with Leeds United, but he arrived at Boundary Park on a free. It seemed that in no time at all he had blossomed into a cultured full-back, and Manchester United manager Alex Ferguson saw in Irwin just what he had been seeking: a player who could operate in either full-back spot, and one, moreover, who could get forward and strike with deadly effect from free-kick situations. He was, for good measure, a player who seldom had to drop out through injury. And he had an equable temperament. All these qualities added up, of course, when it came to talking business – and it cost Manchester United £750,000 to tempt Oldham to part with him.

Then there was Earl Barrett, a £35,000 signing by Joe Royle from Manchester City. Barrett, a genuine athlete who is fleet of foot and lithe in his movement, soon demonstrated that he could operate effectively virtually anywhere along the back-four line, and after Ron Atkinson had taken charge at Villa Park he was prompted to inquire about Barrett. Oldham said they would talk business, and a deal was struck at £1.7 million. After Joe Royle had gone to Everton as their manager, he was quick to re-sign Barrett, even though it meant Villa getting their money back. And so the wheel turned full circle for manager and player.

When Ian Marshall moved to Ipswich Town, Oldham received more than seven times the amount – £100,000 – they had paid to Everton for him; and after Andy Goram had joined Oldham on a free transfer from West Brom, he ended up travelling on to Hibernian for £350,000 and, ultimately, to Rangers and a place in the Scotland international side. Along the way, his total transfer value to Oldham worked out at half a million pounds. Joe Royle would have been happy to splash out £1 million for him, had that been possible when Oldham moved up into the Premier League.

Andy Linighan (£45,000), like Denis Irwin, Tommy

Wright (£80,000) and Andy Ritchie (£50,000), arrived at Boundary Park from Leeds United. When Linighan moved on to Norwich City, he brought Oldham £350,000, and he became a £1 million player when he joined Arsenal.

In several instances, the canny Royle worked out transfer deals which involved 'roll-on' payments to Oldham, should the player concerned be sold yet again at a profit. Like Goram, Linighan and Wright brought the Latics extra cash from further deals; Wright left Oldham for Leicester, at £300,000, and later moved to Middlesbrough for double that amount. As for Ritchie, he stayed at Boundary Park for something like eight years, so he amply repaid the £50,000 fee. Indeed, when he was handed a free transfer in the summer of 1995, the fans (with whom he was a tremendous favourite) urged the club not to let him go.

Winger Rick Holden was another bargain buy by Joe Royle; he arrived from Watford as a £150,000 investment. Manchester City tempted Oldham's manager to say 'yes' to a deal which took Holden to Maine Road. It was one in which Oldham valued Holden at £900,000, and they chucked in £300,000 to secure two players, Steve Redmond and Neil Pointon, who together were rated at £1.2 million. Not so long afterwards, Joe Royle was talking again to Manchester City. This time he finished up re-signing Rick Holden for a more modest fee than his original price tag. Holden's return trip cost Oldham £350,000. Good business, all this, whichever way you looked at it.

Royle went shopping abroad, too, when he landed Gunnar Halle, who went to the World Cup with Norway in the summer of 1994. Halle was a modestly priced £220,000, and has given Oldham fine service. By the time Joe Royle was on his way to Goodison Park, he had also left behind him a handsome legacy for Oldham Athletic, in the shape of several home-produced players who would command more hefty transfer fees. If Oldham had missed out by rejecting £1 million from Leeds for Richard Jobson, they still had some young footballers who could command a similar amount of cash, such as goalkeeper Paul Gerrard, a regular with the England Under-21 side; midfielder Paul Bernard, capped by Scotland at senior level in 1995; and skipper Nick Henry, a Liverpudlian who was a little dynamo in midfield. Oldham certainly owed Joe Royle a massive vote of thanks for his wheeling and dealing during the dozen years of his stewardship. On one occasion he turned out a team which, I estimated, had cost in total no more than £3.5 million – compare this with the star-studded opposition provided by Manchester United.

Chapter Ten

THE OUTSIDER MOVES IN

There are probably dozens, if not hundreds, of fellows by the name of Peter Johnson scattered around the length and breadth of the British Isles. Come to that, there are probably more than a few Mike Walkers living in Britain, too. As for the Peter Johnson who controls the purse strings at Everton Football Club, he has shown that he is a man who knows what he wants: success. Hence the rise and fall of manager Mike Walker.

When Peter Johnson moved onwards and upwards from Prenton Park, the home of Tranmere Rovers, to Goodison Park, the home of former soccer aristocrats Everton, he got what he wanted in fairly quick time. His arrival turned out to be good news for the Goodison club and its long-suffering supporters. In fact, there was good news and bad news, with the latter coming first as results took a disturbing downswing, which led to the sacking of Walker, then became considerably more upbeat after the hiring of Joe Royle. Everton not only managed to retain their Premiership status; they collected a silver pot to put on the sideboard and give them added cause for celebration.

Peter Johnson is a man who made his mark and his fortune via the business of selling food hampers. By 1995, he was not only Everton's chairman, but being quoted as a man whose wealth exceeded that of David Moores, chairman of

Liverpool Football Club and a member of the multi-millionaire Moores family.

There was an interesting report published in the mid-1990s on the 500 wealthiest people in the country. Peter Johnson was listed as one of those in the very top bracket. Paul McCartney was said to be richer than the entire royal family . . . The survey claimed that another scouser, Paul Raymond, was in the billionaire class, with his sex-magazine empire worth £1.65 billion, and that close behind him came David Sainsbury of the supermarket family, with a fortune of £1.38 billion. Mayfair landlord, the Duke of Westminster, came into the list at a reported £900 million, with Steve Morgan – a Liverpudlian and founder of Redrow Homes – listed in the wealth chart at £216 million.

It was recorded that 'new Everton boss Peter Johnson, at £129 million, is 43 places higher than Liverpool chairman David Moores' – he was given a rating of £91 million. It was reported also that the youngest multi-millionaire to make it into the *Business Age* magazine list was John Lennon's 19-year-old son, Sean, while 'various Moores-clan members are included, with John Moores II at £140 million having the biggest share of the £1.7 billion family wealth'.

If all the figures were correct, they certainly made Everton's new chairman in a position to put a considerable chunk of cash into the club – and, from all accounts, when he took over there was indeed a genuine and urgent need for someone to come to the rescue. Back in May 1993 there had been rumours that Everton was up for sale, although this was refuted at the time. Yet the speculation continued, because there were continuing reports that the club was strapped for cash to sign new players.

The then chairman, Dr David Marsh, issued a statement virtually dismissing suggestions that the club's major shareholder, 97-year-old Sir John Moores, was about to unload his controlling interest, although one story did say: 'It is understood that the Moores family have instructed merchant bankers Hill Samuel to investigate ways of refinancing the club, and a buy-out of their stake is seen as the most straightforward option.' In the course of time, and after a somewhat protracted takeover battle, it was not Everton director Bill Kenwright – rated the favourite to gain control – but Peter Johnson who emerged as the man with the power.

While Kenwright was being described as 'the head of a showbusiness empire', Johnson was labelled the 'outsider', the 'multi-millionaire chairman of Tranmere Rovers', and it was being recorded that 'decisions are now being taken to resolve the unsatisfactory situation over control of a club now £4 million in debt'. Sir John Moores, whom I had known for more than 30 years, had just died, and when his will was published it was revealed that his 40 per cent holding in Everton (always his first love, although he had a 25 per cent stake in Liverpool as well) had been divided equally between his sons, Peter and John. The same applied to Sir John's Liverpool shareholding.

One story related that Peter and John Moores 'look certain to sell their shares, and Kenwright and Johnson have already made presentations to accountants acting for the brothers'. According to a report, Sir John Moores' 40 per cent holding was worth around £4 million, and John Moores junior had said only recently that 'my shares are for sale, but I could use them to make things work for the right man. I'm looking for someone to put money in, and if he is okay I'll use my shareholding to get behind him. An investor must have Everton Football Club at heart. Cash is needed at Everton.' He could say that again. Indeed, the Moores brothers were being urged either to sell out, or to inject money into the club themselves.

Peter Parry, who was chairman of the Everton shareholders' association, had his say about things: 'They must either utilise these shares and make them an asset to Everton, or get rid of them. In Bill Kenwright you have a True

Blue who is Everton through to his boots. I have great respect for his love of the club.' On the other hand, as Parry also said, 'Peter Johnson is a man who has the capital and the drive to do the things we want. Either of these two charismatic characters could put Everton back where they should be.' Meaning right up there, along with Manchester United and Liverpool.

Oddly enough, it was just after Everton had gone to Boundary Park and inflicted a 1-0 defeat upon Joe Royle's Oldham Athletic that things began to hot up on the takeover front, as Everton and their supporters awaited the return – and the turn of events – of Peter Johnson, who had embarked upon a cruise in the Aegean. He was 'a long-time Liverpool fan and shareholder who had rescued Tranmere Rovers from oblivion six years ago, but is now concerned that their support does not match his ambition as chairman for a Premiership place'.

Johnson, it was said, 'had talks earlier in the summer [this was now October 1993, the month after the death of Sir John Moores] with representatives of the Moores family and their nominees, who control 50 per cent of the 2,500 Everton shares. He spoke by phone yesterday with friend Frank Corfe, vice-chairman and chief executive at Tranmere, and the situation should be clarified after their meeting tonight'. Then this question was posed: 'Could it be the most significant transfer between the two clubs [Tranmere and Everton] since Dixie Dean's £3,000 move in 1925?' It was pointed out that Everton, £4 million in debt, 'need a big cash injection if they are to regain their position among the game's major powers. In their latest transfer activity they have taken striker Brett Angell on approval from Southend. The 25-year-old is on a month's loan, with a £1.2 million fee agreed if he satisfies.'

It was further reported that 'one pleasing sign was continuing evidence that the penny has finally dropped for Peter Beagrie, the winger who flattered and frustrated but could have arrived as a real force at the age of 27'. It was recorded that 'manager Howard Kendall was one of those who often fumed at Beagrie's failure to deliver from promising positions he created for himself – in fact, it always seemed the £750,000 buy he inherited from predecessor Colin Harvey was about to be shown the Goodison exit'. In fact, Beagrie, like Kendall, did make his exit from Goodison Park – he became a £1 million signing by Manchester City, the club which, with great reluctance in the end, had seen Kendall leave Maine Road and return to Goodison.

Meanwhile, the takeover finally came about, with Johnson emerging as the supremo in the July and things going smoothly. This state of affairs wasn't to last for long, though, because after Kendall's departure and the arrival of Mike Walker, Everton had to endure a roller-coaster ride which was fraught with problems for the club and its new manager. Right the way through, though, it has to be said that Mike Walker gave no indication that he was ready to push the panic button, as the going got tougher and tougher. Maybe he had learned something from his earlier days when results had gone badly for the team he had first managed. For instance, he had his failures as well as his successes during his spell as Norwich City's team boss. He saw Blackburn Rovers hammer his side 7-1, and then the Canaries went visiting again and found themselves 'submitting to a 3-0 mugging at Wimbledon'. Walker's reaction: 'I'm not panicking. My hair is grey enough now – I'm not going to start tearing it out. If we had panicked after the beating at Blackburn we wouldn't be in the position we're in now.' At that time, Norwich City were still in contention for the Championship trophy.

Walker himself emerged as a candidate for the Everton job after having put Norwich on the map, not least when he masterminded their qualification for the UEFA Cup and saw his team achieve a famous victory over Bayern Munich. As a player, he had been a goalkeeper, although his son, Ian, achieved greater fame when he ousted Norway's World Cup keeper, Eric Thorstvedt, from the first team at Tottenham Hotspur and became a contender for an England place. Mike Walker's first managerial spell saw him in charge of Colchester United, but that job lasted no more than 12 months. At Norwich, he worked for five years with the reserves before being elevated, to the surprise of many people, to the manager's job at Carrow Road in 1992.

It wasn't long before folk were sitting up and taking notice, as the Canaries – always regarded as one of the game's footballing clubs – contrived to make a bid not only for the Championship, but for glory in the European arena. Along the way, Walker made his mark and, when the Everton job was going, it became clear that he would certainly be interested. It was suggested in some quarters that he wasn't getting the cash backing he felt was required to turn Norwich into one of the top clubs, able to compete on level terms with the so-called glamour outfits, and ultimately he left Carrow Road to try to resurrect the fortunes of Everton. Norwich were extremely unhappy about his departure, and they complained to the powers-that-be; and while Everton denied having broken or even bent the rules concerning an approach, and Walker himself agreed with his new employers, the Canaries made it clear they wanted compensation.

Everton and Mike Walker did go into partnership – his achievement at Norwich had made him 'a natural choice to succeed Howard Kendall', and he went into action at the start of 1994. In his first match as Everton's team boss, Walker enjoyed a spectacular success at Goodison Park, watching as his new team went out and hammered hapless Swindon Town 6-2. Not so long afterwards, he was 'looking forward to the big one' – the 150th Merseyside derby game, which was scheduled to take place at Anfield. It was reported that Everton were going to meet Liverpool with their confidence 'reinforced by a cluster of four Premiership matches without defeat. It has helped to put a healthy distance between themselves and the relegation zone.'

Those four matches, however, were all at home – in fact, five of their last six Premiership matches had been played at Goodison Park. The Anfield derby game then loomed as the first of seven away games which Everton had to tackle in their last eleven fixtures. So far that season they had won only three times on other grounds. So a good start was important, especially since Walker would then have to go on to face a more personal derby at Norwich. Everton lost that encounter 3-0. Before that, though, the Anfield derby game also turned out to be a disappointment for Mike Walker, in that Everton went down by the odd goal in three. This was the last derby game to be played in front of the famous Kop, and Liverpool's old master-marksman on such occasions, Ian Rush, added another derby-game goal to his tally (25 in 32 derbies), while newcomer Robbie Fowler was the match-winner. Walker's disappointment was all the greater, because he had seen his own centre-half, Dave Watson, head Everton into the lead after only 20 minutes – but Rush smashed in an instant equaliser. (Ironically, both Rush and Fowler had started out as fans of the Goodison club, while Watson, once a Liverpool reserve-team player, had made his mark after leaving Anfield for Carrow Road in a £100,000 transfer.)

On that derby-game day – Sunday, 13 March 1994 – Everton stood nine places from the foot of the table, with 31 matches behind them, while Liverpool (under new management, also, after the departure of Graeme Souness and the appointment of long-serving Roy Evans) were seventh from the top. Joe Royle's Oldham Athletic, having escaped relegation by the skin of their teeth in the previous season, were three places from the bottom and, as events turned out, were doomed to go down. No one realised that Sunday that Everton themselves would be playing out a last-day drama with the accent very much on Premiership survival.

The previous January, the great Sir Matt Busby had died, and it fell to Everton to visit Old Trafford shortly afterwards. Before that game, a minute's silence was observed as people stood in memory of Sir Matt. 'Their fans were a genuine credit in the manner of their respectful silence, and the team is beginning to come to terms with a manager whose tolerance threshold is extremely low. It will not take Mike Walker long to squeeze out any malingerers and bring in players who have a genuine respect for the Everton tradition and share his ambitions to restore the club's fortunes.'

Walker observed, after Everton's 1-0 defeat (though not disgrace) that 'Manchester United are the best team in the country by a street'. He went on: 'They showed today what I want my team to pick up on – it is movement off the ball which is so destructive, and that's what we've got to get around to. We have good players at this club, despite what some people think. We had a kick in the teeth losing at home to Bolton in the FA Cup from two-up on Wednesday, but the training was upbeat on Thursday, and the spirit is superb. It needs me to get down to work, press a few of my ideas on them, and we'll turn the corner. I don't see a problem there. We need more competition at the club, especially up front, because we're not flush with forwards. Common sense tells you we need a couple of strikers. I might be able to do a certain amount from within, but it's my job to look, evaluate and then make my decisions.'

By the time Everton travelled across the park in March to tackle Liverpool, relegation was not something that really exercised the minds of the Everton faithful – but it was going to turn out a real cliffhanger as the season came towards its end. By mid-April 1994 Everton had collected 40 points from the 38 matches they had played, and they were looking down upon only five clubs. From the bottom, it was Swindon Town, Sheffield United, Southampton, Oldham Athletic and Tottenham Hotspur, who trailed Mike Walker's team by a single point. Oldham lagged by three points, Southampton were on the 36-point mark, Sheffield United were one point adrift of the Saints, and Swindon were already doomed, with just 26 points to their credit.

The final day of the campaign saw Everton's supporters flocking to Goodison Park for the crucial decider against Wimbledon. Nothing less than outright victory was called for in this crunch game – but when Wimbledon forged a two-goal lead, the Goodison faithful feared the worst. In an astonishing match, however, Everton hauled themselves off the deck and struck back with a goal which gave them fresh heart; and when they equalised the home supporters began to live in hope.

The man who started the ball rolling for Everton was Graham Stuart, signed from Chelsea for £800,000, and when he struck from the penalty spot, he repaid another chunk of that considerable fee. Only one week previously, he had scored his first goal for Everton – as Joe Royle well recalled, it turned out to be the match-winner against Oldham Athletic. And against Wimbledon, he was on the mark not once but twice. As Everton, heartened by Stuart's goal, pressed forward for an equaliser, they gained their reward through Welsh international Barry Horne; and, suddenly, the home supporters were in full cry as they urged their team to even greater deeds. It was Stuart who obliged, as he scored the third and decisive goal; and so, after this nail-biting, last-ditch battle to ensure Premiership status, Everton had come through and survived.

Mike Walker, who had appeared beforehand to be confident that when it came to the crunch, his players could pull off a rescue act, saw his confidence justified. But, like everyone from the boardroom down to the last supporter, he was well aware that if salvation was to be savoured there and then, the Goodison club would be called upon to face a further test in the not-so-distant future. The plain fact was that, having survived, Everton had to demonstrate their ability to make progress and prove that better times were indeed just around the corner. There might be a respite for a couple of months or so, but with the start of the next season the contest would resume all over again. And next time, the team had got to start winning matches on a regular basis. Walker himself recognised that for him, the next few months could turn out to be make or break; should Everton go forward, his reputation as a team boss would be enhanced. But if the downward slide continued, his job could very well be in jeopardy.

Three matches into season 1994-95 and the portents for Everton were not good. Newcastle United, Blackburn Rovers and Manchester United were lording it at the top of the Premiership table, while down at the bottom (reading upwards) it was Leicester City, Coventry City, and then Everton. Leicester, newly promoted, had still to pick up their first point; Coventry and Everton, like West Ham United immediately above them, had just one point apiece. And Manchester City manager Brian Horton was celebrating, with a feeling of satisfaction no doubt mixed with some relief, the first anniversary of his arrival at Maine Road.

City had just played host to Everton, and scored a resounding 4-0 victory which took them into sixth spot, immediately behind Liverpool; indeed, there was talk of a City challenge to Manchester United's supremacy, if not the Championship itself. Before the season was over, the storm clouds had gathered over Maine Road and Goodison Park, and both Manchester City and Everton were in the market for new managers. The Maine Road match report related how former Liverpool striker Paul Walsh and German counterpart Uwe Rosler had each scored a brace of goals to ensure 'an emphatic defeat of troubled Everton'. Horton, it was said, had been 'under pressure for most of his year at Maine Road, but City played with such spirit and confidence, especially once they had turned their domination into goals, that their fans are convinced happier times are ahead'.

And Everton? 'Sadly, there is presently less cause to view

the new era at Goodison with similar optimism. Mike Walker's side seldom created any serious problems and, on this evidence, the promised signing of Nigerian World Cup striker Daniel Amokachi will be hardly sufficient to fire a revival without other purchases. City outshone their rivals in every department, but the constant early threat from Rosler and Peter Beagrie failed to pay off until after the break.' Then the goals flowed for City. 'Everton's only serious efforts,' it was recorded, 'were set up by £2.2 million newcomer Vinny Samways [purchased from Tottenham Hotspur] in the first half. Unfortunately, John Ebbrell headed straight at Tony Coton, while later Keith Curle just managed to deflect a Samways cross beyond Paul Rideout's reach.'

Samways' future at Everton was later to be called into question, as was the future of Rideout, and the same applied to Amokachi after he had arrived as a £3 million reinforcement. By the beginning of October, when Everton had five matches under their belt, the situation was looking even more gloomy than it had after the defeat at Maine Road. By the time folk on Merseyside were starting to think about the derby game which was scheduled for Goodison Park the following month, Everton – with those five games played – were propping up all the other clubs in the Premiership. Their three draws constituted a less-than-satisfactory return from their expensive investment in players.

Twelve days before the Goodison derby game, Liverpool were looking ahead from fifth spot in the table and being urged to heed a warning. 'While Everton have made a disastrous start to the season, the Reds will travel equipped with the knowledge that a tough game lies ahead. Our neighbours have made the worst start in their distinguished history, and occupy bottom place. But players and supporters will acknowledge the fact that Mersey derbies have nothing to do with form and League placings. Earlier conquests, earlier disappointments, are all forgotten when red and blue line up and one city's pride is at stake. Everton have established, recognised players who have been tested and proved over previous hurdles. They have Duncan Ferguson from Rangers [another costly acquisition in the future, at £4 million, after an initial loan spell], who will enjoy the special atmosphere and the first experience of a big game where supporters of both clubs travel together. It will be the 151st derby, and the rivalry will be as intense as ever. Passion can overtake the form books. Everton won the corresponding game 2-0 last season, Liverpool won 2-1 at Anfield.'

By the time that 21 November had come round, Mike Walker was no longer in charge of team affairs at Goodison Park. He had been sacked, and the talk was that he would be seeking a pay-off of around £450,000 for the remaining part of his contract. Walker had been Everton's manager for only ten months, during which time he had seen his side win no more than half a dozen matches out of the 35 they had played. And in the 14 games which had been played during season 1994-95, Everton could show just one victory and eight points – relegation form, if it continued. As Walker moved out, Joe Royle admitted that he believed his chance of ever returning to Goodison Park as 'the boss' had vanished. But now he was back, and saying he had arrived 'with an open mind'. A big fellow physically, Joe Royle wasn't afraid to accept the challenge from Peter Johnson of putting distance between Everton and the threat of relegation from the Premiership. However, he couldn't have faced a more demanding test than the one which was offered straight away: the 151st derby game against Liverpool.

Chapter Eleven

A ROYLE REPRIEVE

Joe Royle began season 1994-95 as the manager of a team which had been relegated from the Premiership, and ended it as the manager of a team which had secured Premiership survival and gone on to win the FA Cup. His predecessor, Mike Walker, had paid the penalty at Everton although, to the surprise of many people, the axe fell upon Walker just after he had seen his side start to claw back some precious points. True, Everton were still not in the business of winning matches, but they had managed several draws in their unbeaten run and that appeared to suggest better times ahead. Indeed, they had just picked up five points out of nine.

As for Joe Royle, in between his unsuccessful mission to inspire Oldham Athletic to a Houdini escape act for the second season on the trot and his trip to Wembley as Everton's season-saving manager, he had come through some sticky moments as well as savouring some high points. He underwent a baptism of fire in his first match in charge, the Goodison Park confrontation with Liverpool. It was a game which the home side won, to give their new manager a flying start. At last, Everton's League season came to life, as Duncan Ferguson, the lanky striker on loan from Rangers, rose above the Liverpool defence to power a header past David James and thus get his name on the Everton scoresheet for the first time. 'He went to war,' declared Joe Royle; and in some quarters after that Everton's team became known as 'The Dogs of War'. It was a slip by James which gave Paul Rideout the opportunity to make the scoreline 2-0 for Everton, and that morale-boosting victory also lifted them off the bottom of the table.

Nevertheless, Premiership survival was not achieved without one or two alarms and excursions along the way, such as narrow defeats against Leeds United and Blackburn Rovers. On both occasions Everton were adjudged to have been somewhat unfortunate to have come out of those matches without a point to their name. In the latter, the Rovers had to scrap grimly for the points which boosted their tally as they chased the Championship. Blackburn's 2–1 victory at Goodison Park moved them six points clear at the top of the table after goals from their costly strikers, Alan Shearer and Chris Sutton, in the first seven minutes of the game set the Rovers on the path to success. Dalglish may have been less than impressed by the manner in which the win was achieved, however, as he said: 'We didn't play up to the standards we have set ourselves.' The critics tended to agree with him, too – but, as the Rovers' manager also pointed out: 'At this stage of the season, points are more important than performance.' This was a view which was echoed fervently by Joe Royle, although for different reasons – that defeat sent Everton spinning back into the relegation zone.

Shearer and Sutton by then had collected 46 goals between them (31 for Shearer), and Royle must dearly have wished he had the pair as his strike force. Yet he could take some comfort from the manner in which his own players battled back after the early shock of those goals. 'They caught us cold. The front two of Sutton and Shearer are a real handful, and once they had put Blackburn two goals ahead it was always going to be hard for us.' Dalglish, rating his side fortunate to be going home with the points, said of

Everton: 'I think they must be disappointed that they didn't get something from the game. We had some good fortune around the goalmouths, and I hope our luck stays with us until the end of the season.' The home fans showed their feelings by deriding Blackburn at the end, while giving their own team a standing ovation.

Even so, there came a warning for the Goodison outfit: 'Everton may well be in for another dramatic finale before Premiership survival is assured.' And certainly there were no easy matches for Joe Royle's team. Apart from Liverpool, Leeds United away and Blackburn Rovers at home, the Blues had to tackle high-riding Newcastle United – who were aiming at least for a place in Europe – and Championship-chasing Manchester United; not to mention a second joust with their Merseyside rivals, this time at Anfield. Everton also faced hard matches away against Ipswich Town and Coventry City, both clubs needing points in their own fight for survival.

Manchester United went to Goodison Park on the back of a stirring FA Cup success and a good result at Carrow Road. United, indeed, had set about Leeds at Old Trafford to such good effect that they did a demolition job on Howard Wilkinson's team, and then they travelled to East Anglia and inflicted a 2-0 midweek defeat upon Mike Walker's former club. Joe Royle was moved to express his admiration for United in a single word: 'awesome'. Yet when United did arrive at Goodison, they discovered that there would be no easy pickings for them, because the 'Dogs of War' set about devouring the opposition.

Royle had described the defeat at Elland Road as a hiccup, saying: 'That was our best away performance since I came to the club.' He also said that the Elland Road reverse made the Goodison Park confrontation with Manchester United 'a massive game for both clubs. We know we're up against a terrific team – probably the finest in modern times and one capable of doing the double double. They were awesome against Leeds in the Cup, and we have to make sure we don't make the same mistake of giving them early goals.' Everton didn't; instead, they struck first, and it proved to be the only goal of the game. Their marksman was the controversial Duncan Ferguson. Afterwards, he received a handsome tribute from Everton's manager: 'He could be the biggest thing here since Dixie Dean. I have never seen a player receive as much adulation in such a short time. He is the man the punters all want to see, and he's looking pretty cheap at the moment, even at £4 million.'

The game had been going just under an hour when Ferguson struck with a devastating header; and to celebrate, as the Everton fans roared their relief, he whipped off his jersey and whirled it round in triumph. That goal brought to an end Manchester United's impressive run of 13 games in which they had gone unbeaten, including five victories in succession. It was a defeat which ended a sad and sorry week for United manager Alex Ferguson, who the previous day had learned that the Football Association had increased the club's suspension on the disgraced Eric Cantona, after his kung-fu act at Selhurst Park.

Ferguson could console himself to some extent by the fact that Blackburn Rovers had dropped two points in their home game, but he knew well enough that his own front men, Mark Hughes and £7 million striker Andy Cole, had let Everton off the hook on more than one occasion. Twice Cole had been presented with scoring chances, only to fail when he was left with just Neville Southall to beat. Having snapped up a long ball from Denis Irwin, Cole followed the hard bit by snatching at his shot – and as he saw the ball go a foot wide, he registered his disgust by thumping the ground. Then, just before Ferguson struck, Paul Ince and Ryan Giggs played a one-two which presented Cole with another opening. This time, the striker found Neville Southall barring the way to goal with his outstretched legs.

Southall also managed to foil Hughes as he stuck out a

foot to block a close-range effort, and United's failure to take their chances proved costly as the play ebbed and flowed, with neither side asking for nor giving quarter as the tackles went in. Everton might have gone ahead before Ferguson's goal, because the Scot set up John Ebbrell for a shot, but Ebbrell chipped the ball over the bar. However, when Everton won a corner in the 58th minute, Andy Hinchcliffe was spot-on as he slipped the ball goalwards. It curled in dangerously from the right-hand corner flag, and there was Ferguson, lurking at the far post. He soared above the United defenders and buried the ball, with Peter Schmeichel helpless. Minutes later, Schmeichel contrived to make a desperate save on the goal-line to prevent Hinchcliffe scoring directly from a corner kick. Alex Ferguson and Joe Royle each had their own views on the game afterwards.

United's manager declared: 'There's a long way to go yet. I thought we deserved it. Our best chances fell to our strikers – we had five, and had we scored one, we'd have gone on and won it.' Well, United didn't; and Royle summed up: 'The results have gone our way, and the lads are up for it in the dressing-room. There's no room for complacency; we've got to keep our feet on the ground.'

When it came to taking on Liverpool the second time around, Everton held their rivals to a scoreless draw at Anfield and drew some pointed criticism from Liverpool manager Roy Evans. Naturally, Evans had offered Joe Royle and his team a warm welcome to Anfield and, as usual, given his own players and fans a warning to expect a hard game. But afterwards, Evans demonstrated that he was not happy either with the refereeing of Brian Hill or with the manner in which Everton had disrupted his own side's passing game. 'If anybody ever mentions the School of Science to me again, I'm sorry – I don't see it,' he declared, shaking his head. This, of course, was a reference to the proud claim of the Goodison Park fans going back over the years.

Evans further declared: 'I am frustrated and angry. We

tried to play attacking football with fluency, but were not given the protection. Every time we got past their back four we were hacked down. Okay – the referee took four names in the first half, but why didn't he continue in the second half? I don't like to see people getting sent off, but we were stopped from playing football.' Joe Royle had his point of view, of course. 'I'm disappointed that in the first half the bookings went one way. I can't argue with the bookings that were given, but I thought they should have been balanced out.'

Everton had followed the same tactics they had employed in the game against Liverpool at Goodison Park. They had succeeded in halting Liverpool's attempts to play their own style of football and, in the process, had gone close enough to chalking up their first derby game double in a decade. With the final minutes ticking away, it was Duncan Ferguson rising to meet a cross from John Ebbrell, only to see David James foil him. And in the last few seconds Ferguson almost clinched victory as he rammed a left-footer goalwards. But his shot rose just over the bar.

Liverpool, it was said, 'tried to meet fire with fire', and referee Hill, according to one report, 'showed leniency to them' as he booked only their £3 million Irish international defender, Phil Babb, while jotting down the names of four Everton players (Dave Watson, Joe Parkinson, David Burrows and David Unsworth) in his notebook. Neither keeper was called upon to perform heroics – Southall blocked a close-range shot from John Scales, James made two comfortable saves from Duncan Ferguson and Barry Horne, in turn.

Liverpool's disappointment was heightened by the fact that they had won only one of their last five matches (a Coca-Cola Cup-tie against Arsenal) while Everton had the satisfaction of knowing that since Joe Royle's arrival they had climbed from the foot of the table to 16th place. But their manager still spelled it out for his players, as he declared: 'We have to have that spirit all the time. So many sides come here and lie down – we certainly were not going to do that. I thought we might have nicked it at the end, although that would probably have been a bit harsh on Liverpool.'

Harsh or not, the fact remained that Everton had prised a valuable point from their Merseyside rivals, and every point counted in the battle to stay up. By the time Everton were coming towards the close of the season, they were promising success on two fronts, because in the FA Cup they were on their way to Wembley, while in the League it seemed they would finally break free of the relegation shackles. Even so, there were some tricky fixtures at the tail-end of the campaign, although by then Ipswich Town were virtually down and out, while Coventry City, under new manager Ron Atkinson, had edged towards safety and then found themselves under pressure again.

At last, though, Everton accomplished their first mission successfully when they travelled to Portman Road and scored the only goal of the game. There was a touch of irony in the fact that Paul Rideout, whose future under Howard Kendall and Mike Walker at Goodison had looked unsure, had found new belief as Royle gave him free rein, and it was he who struck the goal which meant so much to Everton.

By the time Everton went to Highfield Road for their final League game, Coventry City had achieved safety, and the scoreless draw was probably a predictable result. Both Joe Royle and Ron Atkinson could smile and congratulate each other on having achieved their respective missions, while in Everton's case they were free to concentrate upon one more match: their meeting with Manchester United in the FA Cup final on 20 May at Wembley. Everton's three previous final appearances had ended in heartache – beaten by Manchester United in 1985 and by Liverpool in 1986 and 1989. More than that, when Royle was manager of Oldham Athletic, Manchester United had stopped the Latics in their tracks twice at the semi-final stage of the competition.

So, at the end of season 1994-95, the stage was set for a tough duel between sides managed by Joe Royle and Alex Ferguson. Everton could point to a good track-record against the men from Old Trafford, and they had already beaten them once in the League to dent their hopes of retaining the Championship trophy. Now Everton had the opportunity to deny Manchester United the FA Cup, which they had won 12 months previously. The question was: could Joe Royle's men manage to do it?

Chapter Twelve

SEMI-CONSCIOUS!

If losing an FA Cup final is one of the worst things a player can experience (and managers, as well as footballers, will tell you that this is so), then losing an all-Merseyside semi-final must be the bitter end. Alan Ball, having become a manager, reflected upon the derby games in which he used to be involved as an Everton player, and was moved to observe: 'I would give 15 years of my life to play in one again.' Ball's transfer to Arsenal meant that he also played in London derby duels, but he reckoned that these 'were not in the same league as Merseyside matches. The mornings of those meetings reminded me of Christmas as a kid – the excitement and build-up were almost unbearable. It is the supporters of both clubs who make these games what they are – the people of the city create that very special stage.'

Bally was just 17 years of age when he went to Anfield and played in a winning team there (in those days he was still with Blackpool) and he claimed: 'It became a lucky ground for me, and not many players can say that. They were wonderful days on Merseyside. I never wanted the 90 minutes to end; yet the fear of losing was there until the closing moments. It was football on a knife-edge. My memories are precious, but one is very painful – we lost 3-2 at Liverpool, after having been 2-0 in front.'

I remember that match, as does Steve Heighway, who

told me it was the game which brought home to him just how much it meant to the fans and players – especially those born on Merseyside – when their team had triumphed in a derby duel. The match in question took place during season 1970-71, and Heighway was afflicted by a searing migraine which, it seemed, would keep him out of the action. But after a spell lying down in a darkened room he declared himself fit to play, and as Liverpool fought back to draw level twice, with Chris Lawler storming in to claim a late winner, there was delight for Steve and his team-mates, misery for Bally and Everton.

Bob Paisley knew all about derby days, too, and he once told me about an occasion when Everton got the upper hand. That was at Goodison Park in October 1978. 'Almost seven years had gone by since our rivals had been able to claim a victory over us. They managed it that day, and they didn't hide their emotions. It was a long time since I'd seen so many Everton scarves flapping so proudly.' There was a sequel to the match, as well, because a couple of days later Bob was talking to someone about the game. 'They told me of an Everton supporter who lived fairly high up in a block of flats. On the day after Everton's win, this true-blue fan had taken out a record, dusted it off and put it on the turntable – and played it time and again until it almost drove the neighbours dippy. It was the Everton "signature tune".' The neighbours put up with it because, as Bob said, 'They understood. It had been a long time since that fan had anything to make a noise about when it came to a derby game.'

When it comes to FA Cup semi-finals, Alan Ball has more than one hard-luck story to tell, because he suffered when Second Division Sunderland knocked Arsenal off the Wembley trail at Hillsborough in 1973. I was there that day, too, and when I went down to the Gunners' dressing-room at the end, all was silent. My first reaction was that I'd missed them. When I opened the door and peered inside, there was

Bally, all alone. He sat on the bench, looking glassy-eyed, as if he couldn't take in the scale of disaster which had befallen his team. I hadn't the heart to do more than murmur 'Hard luck', then I stole silently away. In any event, I doubt if he would have been able to summon up words to describe his emotions.

Everton's route to Old Trafford had taken them along a road which saw them encounter Blackburn Rovers in the third round, at Goodison Park; and then came three more home ties, against Middlesbrough, Derby County and Colchester United, in turn. Everton's luck in being drawn at home each time had their fans eagerly anticipating that this would be their year to go up for the Cup, and they certainly gave their favourites unqualified support. More than 40,000 fans flocked to Goodison for the third-round duel with Blackburn, and they saw Jimmy Husband strike the brace of goals which sent the Rovers spinning out of football's glamour competition.

When Middlesbrough tried conclusions with Everton at Goodison Park, it turned out to be a 3-0 success for the home side, as Henry Newton, Colin Harvey and Joe Royle got their names on the scoresheet; and in the confrontation with Derby County, although there was only a single goal in it, it was struck for Everton by David Johnson. Everton then had clocked up half a dozen goals, and not conceded even one. It was a case of 'Bring on Colchester' – and the neutrals in the game watched with interest to see what the outcome of this tie would be, because Colchester, totally unfancied even though drawn at home, had famously despatched big-guns Leeds United from the FA Cup, earning a reputation as giant-killers.

However, on the day, there was only one team in it: Everton. The visiting side suffered not once but five times over, as the Blues hammered home their goals without reply. The marksmen were Howard Kendall (who scored twice), Joe Royle, Jimmy Husband and Alan Ball. Not surprisingly, the Goodison fans were delighted – and so were Everton, because the team had commanded tremendous support. For each of the Cup-ties against Middlesbrough, Derby County and Colchester, Everton had attracted crowds of more than 53,000, with the match against 'Boro drawing the highest gate, 54,857. In total, more than 200,000 people had watched Everton progress through to the semi-final. And, of course, there was a massive crowd of 63,000 when they came up against Liverpool at Old Trafford. Liverpool supporters had taken over the Stretford End, Evertonians filled the scoreboard end – and it was the Everton brigade who had cause to cheer the loudest when Ball scored inside quarter of an hour.

Two minutes later, Ian Callaghan was giving the Liverpool contingent something to shout about, as he put the ball into the net – but referee Ken Burns ruled out a goal because of a handling offence. So half-time came with Everton still leading 1-0. And the interval gave Bill Shankly a chance to tell his troops something about the way they could save the game. 'You're over-kicking the ball, rushing things too much. Cool it down,' he said.

When it was all over, Shankly told us waiting press: 'Brian Hall hadn't been getting a kick in the first half. I was thinking of sending for the fire brigade to get him a ladder, so that he could reach those high balls we'd been pumping through!'

The second half was different, as Liverpool bore down towards the Stretford End. When Labone pulled a muscle and limped off, after a tackle against John Toshack, he was replaced by Sandy Brown, and in that second half Toshack began to win the aerial duels, Callaghan started to get the better of Keith Newton, and Alun Evans and Steve Heighway began to come into their own. On one occasion Everton were grateful to see Joe Royle, their centre-forward, heading the ball clear off his own line!

Finally, Liverpool got the goal they had been seeking, as Alun Evans rifled home a shot. From that moment, Liverpool had their tails up, and when Brian Hall beat keeper Andy Rankin that was it. Shankly's men were marching on to Wembley (where they lost to Arsenal, despite Steve Heighway having given them the lead in extra time).

The FA Cup was to be Bill Shankly's parting gift to Liverpool when they beat Newcastle United 3-0 in the 1974 final, and under the astute management of Bob Paisley Liverpool went for a unique treble in season 1976-77 . . . the League title, the FA Cup and the European Cup. They missed out on the FA Cup, although they went to Wembley – and that, from an Evertonian point of view, compensated in some small measure for the fact that Liverpool had won their semi-final duel against the old foe from across Stanley Park.

Liverpool and Everton met again in the FA Cup semi-final of 1977. The match was played twice, in fact, both times at Manchester City's Maine Road ground, and on each occasion the referee was Clive 'The Book' Thomas. His decisions, notably in the first encounter, caused controversy, with Everton fans claiming: 'We wuz robbed!' Indeed, as Duncan McKenzie related later, Thomas was the target for jeers at the end of that game and at the start of the replay. 'For my money, he's a good referee, and he handled the matches to the best of his ability and with complete honesty,' recalled Duncan. 'But so many vital issues will always remain a mystery and a point of controversy, for every decision is down to the human element, and the referee has to make split-second judgments.'

Duncan also told me: 'There isn't an Evertonian alive who doesn't believe it should have been Everton going to Wembley to meet Manchester United in the final. That Saturday afternoon belonged to us. We beat Liverpool all ends up, in my book. We even scored a goal which, I am convinced, was a good winner – but it didn't count.'

Liverpool had scored first, and it was an excellent goal from Terry McDermott, who performed a quick double-shuffle, then chipped the ball over the Everton keeper.

McKenzie scored an equaliser when he snapped up a pass from Martin Dobson, but a Jimmy Case header put Liverpool in front again. However, when Bruce Rioch struck an equaliser, Everton were looking increasingly in command and good for a third goal. They thought they had got it, too. This was the McKenzie version: 'The ball was crossed from the left; I nodded it onwards, and Bryan Hamilton took it on his thigh and directed it past Ray Clemence.'

But referee Thomas soon signalled that he wasn't going to allow the goal to stand. And so the arguments started. Had he believed that Hamilton had handled the ball, and not knocked it into the net with his thigh? Or was it an offside decision against the Everton man? Linesman Colin Seel didn't raise his flag to indicate such an offence, but Thomas was adamant that there had been 'an infringement', and so the match ended in a 2-2 draw.

So what, then, was the reason for the goal being disallowed? According to Thomas, it was McKenzie himself who set the ball rolling, because when the ball was passed to Bryan Hamilton, the Everton marksman was offside. Thomas blew his whistle, yet while Hamilton was being mobbed by team-mates, the linesman – seemingly satisfied that a goal had indeed been scored – was on his way back to the halfway line. But the referee ruled that McKenzie was the culprit for having headed the ball on – by the time he produced that final touch, Hamilton was offside.

Everton manager Gordon Lee was giving vent to his feelings by the touchline, but no blame was attached to the linesman for not having seen the final touch. Thomas claimed, with utter certainty, that when viewers watched the TV recording, they would realise that the cameras had proved him to be right. Thomas also declared that he was certain Hamilton had handled the ball in any event, so he would still have disallowed the goal.

According to McKenzie, after that bitter disappointment on the Saturday, Everton's players simply were not in the right frame of mind for the midweek replay. 'Even in the dressing-room beforehand, I sensed that we were like men who had been beaten, and not played the opposition off the park a few days previously. And when our left-back, Micky Pejic, was adjudged to have pushed David Johnson in the box, it became obvious it wasn't going to be our night. Thomas awarded Liverpool a penalty, and Phil Neal made no mistake. Liverpool had their tails up, we were despondent, and they scored two more goals in the second half.'

Referee Thomas also denied Everton's claim for a penalty after a foot-up challenge by Liverpool keeper Ray Clemence on McKenzie; instead, Thomas awarded an indirect free-kick.

So Liverpool went to the final, only to lose to Manchester United, and Clive Thomas remained convinced that his decisions had been correct. He was to be given charge of yet another Merseyside derby in the FA Cup – this time a fourth-round tie in 1980 – and it was one which provoked a great deal of comment even before a ball had been kicked. For a start, Thomas was pressed by the media to offer his thoughts about the duel, and he later admitted that it turned out to be the most difficult match he had ever refereed between Liverpool and Everton.

Having warned his linesmen about the possibility of trouble, Thomas himself soon showed that he would stand no nonsense – Jimmy Case and Everton keeper Martin Hodge became involved in one incident, with Case being ticked off by the referee, who later declared that Graeme Souness was fortunate to have stayed on the field after a fracas involving Everton defender Mick Lyons. That was a match which ended satisfactorily for Everton fans, though, because they saw their side score two of the game's three goals. It was a game in which tempers were always liable to fray, though, and the count of half a dozen bookings reflected this.

Bob Paisley demonstrated that he could take defeat when

he told the local evening paper that Clive Thomas had come out of the game 'with tremendous credit . . . it was a situation which could easily have got out of hand with a lesser man in charge'. Gordon Lee said it was 'a terribly hard game to control, and it took a top man to handle it'. And my colleague at *The People*, Norman Wynne, wrote: 'Only the firm handling of referee Thomas stopped the game from falling apart.'

During the mid-1980s, Liverpool and Everton tangled again in the FA Cup. This time it was indeed an historic occasion, because they met for the first time in a final at Wembley and Ian Rush, the man who overtook the legendary Dixie Dean's scoring tally in derby games, proved yet again that he could be a bogeyman for the Blues as he scored two goals in Liverpool's 3-1 victory. It was a final which gave the 98,000 crowd full value for their money.

The fans inside the stadium had paid more than £1 million for the privilege of watching the final, and it was estimated that thousands more were locked outside – they had to be satisfied with listening to the match commentary on their radios. Everton were relieved when centre-back Derek Mountfield gave them the all-clear with regard to his fitness, but Liverpool suffered a late pre-match setback when defender Gary Gillespie went down with a stomach virus and Kenny Dalglish reported that he was 'too weak this morning to be available for selection'. So Mark Lawrenson wore the No. 2 shirt, as he teamed up again with Alan Hansen at the heart of the defence.

Though Liverpool appeared to settle more quickly, it was Everton who struck first, with the game less than half an hour old. That wily old midfield player, Peter Reid, delivered a pass which gave Gary Lineker the chance to go streaking clear of Hansen, and while Bruce Grobbelaar went desperately close to saving, he could only parry the ball, and this gave Lineker a second bite at the cherry. He made no mistake, even though the Liverpool keeper got a touch to the ball once more. The Everton fans cheered Lineker's 40th goal of the season.

Liverpool were still fighting to make their mark on the game as the second half got under way, but it was Everton who were pressing forward, and it seemed as if they might well achieve their aim and score a second goal which, surely, would have been a killer. Yet Liverpool pegged away and, as the minutes passed, they survived – even when Everton looked certain to score. It was Grobbelaar to the rescue as he produced a breathtaking save, to push a goal-bound header from Graeme Sharp over the bar. That save, it was said later, marked a turning point in the game.

Liverpool, encouraged, gradually began to find their rhythm; and with almost an hour gone, they got the goal they were seeking as Jan Molby stabbed the ball through the Everton defence for Ian Rush to pounce. His speed took him onwards and past several defenders, so that it became a one-on-one situation: Rush versus keeper Bobby Mimms. And the fans of both sides waited breathlessly to see who would come off best.

Everton's goalkeeper came out, hoping to narrow the angle and create problems for the striker, but Rush was ready for him. He dragged the ball round Mimms and, from the left-hand side of the goal, drove in an angled shot which looked a goal all the way. And it was. At that moment, with Liverpool on a high, everyone inside Wembley sensed that the double was there for the taking . . . and so it proved.

Little more than five minutes after the strike by Rush, Molby was in the thick of the action again as he won possession of the ball, then beat a couple of defenders before sending a pass out square to the right, where Craig Johnston was waiting. He had the time and the space, and he wasted neither; he simply came boring in, then he slotted the ball past the despairing Mimms from close range.

Everton gave Adrian Heath – a goal-poacher on many previous occasions – a chance to show that he could produce something for the Blues, but though he and his team-mates managed to exert some pressure, Liverpool no longer looked vulnerable. The damage had been done. Having survived a 'wobble', drawn level and taken the lead, Liverpool were not about to let their great rivals off the hook.

With less than ten minutes to go, they erased all doubt about the destination of the FA Cup. A three-man move was the clincher, involving Molby, then Ronnie Whelan and Rush. From the left-hand side of the pitch, Whelan lifted his head and spotted Rush, then he swept the ball across to the Welsh international, who wasted no time – he struck his shot firmly, and it sped past Mimms to the far corner of the net.

Rush even had the chance to walk off the Wembley pitch as a hat-trick hero, but though he did everything right, this time Mimms prevented a goal. The chance came when Rush broke clear, and he attempted to chip the ball over the keeper, but Mimms managed to pluck the ball out of the air and deny the Liverpool marksman a third goal. The result meant that Liverpool had come from behind in the League and the Cup to triumph, leaving Everton runners-up in both competitions.

Everton were to suffer again, as they tried conclusions again with Liverpool in the 1989 FA Cup final, the year of the Hillsborough disaster. After that tragic day, Liverpool officials had agonised whether or not to pull out of the FA Cup competition, but in the end they decided to carry on, and after victory over Nottingham Forest in the semi-final which was switched to Old Trafford, the Wembley date meant another encounter with Everton, who had despatched Norwich City at Villa Park on the day of the Hillsborough disaster.

So on Saturday, 20 May, 82,000 fans were inside Wembley as the teams from Merseyside lined up to do battle. The stadium was a cauldron, too, as the temperature soared towards 90 degrees – and it shot even higher when, with only four minutes gone on the clock, Steve Nicol began a move which was helped on by Steve McMahon, who steered the ball to John Aldridge – and the striker who had missed a penalty against Wimbledon at Wembley 12 months previously drilled the ball past Neville Southall.

By half-time Aldridge could easily have been a hat-trick marksman, while Liverpool might well have been four goals ahead, since they had created several clear-cut chances and dominated the first 45 minutes. Everton manager Colin Harvey needed to give his side a real half-time pep-talk.

Yet as the second half wore on, Liverpool clung to their single-goal lead, although Everton forced their way back into the game; and with mere seconds remaining, they managed to make the breakthrough. The move involved centre-back Dave Watson, and it was finished off by substitute Stuart McCall, who scored from close range. One hand on the Cup? Liverpool had to think again!

By then, Ian Rush had replaced Aldridge, and after five minutes in the first period of extra time he struck, collecting a pass and swivelling on a sixpence before releasing a right-footer which curled into the top right-hand corner of the net. But as Liverpool appeared to have snatched a winner, the all-action man, McCall, hammered in a 25-yarder to put Everton level again.

With Everton fans thinking their team might just nick it, Rush did the business for Liverpool once more, this time steering a header past his international team-mate, Neville Southall. And it was all over then.

The FA Cup trail for Liverpool in 1991 began with a third-round tie against Blackburn Rovers at Ewood Park and ended almost on their own doorstep, across Stanley Park, when they tangled with Everton. And seldom can a Cup duel between the Merseyside rivals have produced more drama. After a 0-0 encounter at Anfield, everyone expected another tight game in the replay at Goodison. How wrong can you be? With its glut of goals, this match remains arguably the most exciting Merseyside Cup duel of all time.

Liverpool struck first, and they led Everton no fewer than four times; yet four times their opponents struck back, to salvage a draw and go into a second replay. Two of Liverpool's goals were scored by Peter Beardsley, one came from Ian Rush (as usual!) and another from John Barnes. On any other day, four goals by Liverpool would have sunk the opposition without trace – but the opposition this time wasn't prepared to surrender.

The Everton heroes turned out to be the striking combination of Tony Cottee and Graeme Sharp. Each man beat Bruce Grobbelaar twice, to ensure that Everton lived to fight again . . . and when Everton won the toss for choice of venue, it meant that the second replay would also take place at Goodison Park, on 27 February. And this time Everton made sure of a win with a goal by Dave Watson – who at one time had been a reserve-team player at Anfield. Watson was one of those local-born players who could claim to have figured in the first teams of both Merseyside clubs (Steve McMahon and Gary Ablett were among a handful of others), while another centre-back with Everton and Liverpool connections was Ian Marshall, managed by Joe Royle at Oldham after having been signed from Goodison Park. In Marshall's case, however, he never played for Liverpool, although at one stage he did go to watch them in action (as a dedicated neutral) and it would be difficult to find many more similar characters on Merseyside! Marshall said: 'I went simply to enjoy the games. I admired Kevin Keegan at Liverpool just as much as Bob Latchford at Everton.' Marshall himself played for North Sefton Boys and for Merseyside Boys but, though his father supported Liverpool, the young soccer hopeful chose to try his luck with Everton, and he spent five years at Goodison Park before being snapped up by Joe Royle at Oldham, where he later sought to become recognised as a striker, rather than as a centre-back. During a five-year stint at Boundary Park he played in both positions, and he savoured Oldham's Second Division

Championship success in season 1990–91. He could also look back upon an occasion when he played for Everton against Liverpool, in the 1–1 Charity Shield draw at Wembley in 1986. By 1995, he was wearing the colours of Ipswich Town – which meant that, as with Everton and Oldham, he still wore a blue jersey – while his first club was back at Wembley and beating Manchester United to carry off the FA Cup. This time, Marshall's former manager, Joe Royle, was Everton's team boss.

Chapter Thirteen

THE CUP THAT CHEERS

More than one team has discovered that the road to Wembley is paved with pitfalls – indeed, it has been known for a club to achieve the dubious distinction of going all the way to the final of the FA Cup and being relegated in the same season. Everton managed to avoid such a disaster in 1994-95, but while they had to do battle all the way to preserve their Premiership status, few would have put money on them not only succeeding in this but in winning the FA Cup as well. One punter who was bold enough to place a bet on Everton for the Cup did so at odds of 33–1, which showed what the bookies thought of their chances.

Everton's last victory in an FA Cup final had been achieved 11 years previously in 1984, when, under the management of Howard Kendall, they had beaten Watford 2–0 with goals from Graeme Sharp and Andy Gray. In the third round of the FA Cup competition, in January 1995, they were paired with First Division Derby County, who had aspirations of gaining promotion to the Premiership. Lionel Pickering had spent several million pounds in trying to restore Derby's fortunes, and while they were not pulling up too many trees, they still represented a formidable challenge to Everton, struggling as they were in the top flight. The one thing in Everton's favour was that the tie would be played at Goodison Park. Derby arrived and soon declared their intention of getting through – or, at least, taking Everton back to the Baseball Ground for a replay. But the Blues weathered the County attacks and, in the end, were grateful that left-back Andy Hinchcliffe was able to produce a winner amid cheers of relief from the home spectators. While victory was welcomed also by Joe Royle, he would still have been ready at that stage to swap success for three League points.

The fourth round paired Everton with one of Royle's former clubs, Bristol City, and the tie was to be played at Ashton Gate. It was not one to which any top-flight club, struggling or otherwise, could look forward. For instance, one half of Merseyside still harboured nightmare memories of what had happened to Liverpool the previous season when, after drawing away, they had tried conclusions with the men from Bristol at Anfield. Brian Tinnion had not only scored Bristol's winner but his goal effectively brought to an end the reign of Graeme Souness as Liverpool's manager. Victory for City over Everton at Ashton Gate wouldn't see off Joe Royle, of course, but it would not do his or his team's confidence any good.

The pitch was little better than a mud-heap as Everton and their opponents got down to it, and it soon became apparent that the home players were not just there to make up the numbers. Bristol battered away at the Everton defence, and it began to look as if Joe Royle's team might well be bowing out of the FA Cup and talking about 'concentrating on the League'. In the event, it was a goal against the run of play which marked a turning point in the match as right-back Matt Jackson produced a stunning 25-yard volley which fairly sizzled goalwards. Some of the Goodison faithful who had made the trip to Ashton Gate were ready there and then to vote this their goal of the season. Jackson, indeed, said later that with Everton under so much pressure, he had whacked the ball with the idea of hitting it on to the roof of the stand, to give his team some relief! That, no doubt, was a bit of tongue-in-cheek humour. At any rate, it won the tie.

So Everton awaited the draw for the fifth round, and they learned that they would be back on home ground – with a piquant pairing, in that the visitors would be Norwich City. Once again, this was a club for which Joe Royle had played while, of course, Norwich had been less than happy when Everton had signed up their manager, Mike Walker. But on this occasion there was no room for argument, because Everton managed to produce a scintillating performance which had the Canaries on the rack. Joe Parkinson struck to register his first goal for the Goodison club; then came four more strikes, as Anders Limpar, Duncan Ferguson, Paul Rideout and Graham Stuart each got their name on the scoresheet. Result: Everton 5, Norwich City 0. And now, with a quarter-final tie in sight, the scent of Wembley was in the air.

Once again, fortune favoured Joe Royle and his team, as the draw for the sixth round gave them home advantage although the opposition, in the shape of Kevin Keegan's Newcastle United, promised that this would be a tough one. Keegan's team had kicked off the season in tremendous form and had led the way at the top of the table for weeks; they were also hotly fancied by many people to wind up at Wembley in the FA Cup, even if by the time of the sixth round their title aspirations had been virtually snuffed out. This, decided the BBC, was undoubtedly the match of the round, and so the television cameras were focused on Goodison Park. The action was fast and furious, and the issue was decided by a single goal. Once again, as he had done in the third-round tie against Derby County, Andy Hinchcliffe played a key role, this time planting a free-kick perfectly for Duncan Ferguson to get a touch with his head. The ball went on to skipper Dave Watson, who guided it past the keeper.

And so it was on to the semi-finals, with the draw

featuring Manchester United, Crystal Palace and Tottenham Hotspur. By general consent, the 'dream final' would be United versus Spurs, Jurgen Klinsmann and all – and when the pairings were made, it was Everton who had to tackle Tottenham and United who must meet Palace yet again, after their ill-starred duel at Selhurst Park in the January which had led to Eric Cantona being banned. So the dream final looked on.

Everton and Tottenham kicked off first, in their semi-final at Elland Road, which had not always been a happy hunting ground for Joe Royle during his Oldham days. Spurs, not surprisingly, were rated the favourites, as were Manchester United in their tie; but Everton made a nonsense of all that as they took the semi-final by the scruff of the neck and shook Spurs almost until they rattled. Tottenham's destiny, many people believed, was to go all the way to Wembley; after all, they had first been barred from competing in the FA Cup competition during season 1994-95, then reprieved just in time for them to play in the third round. But revelling in their 'Dogs of War' tag, the men from the so-called Goodison School of Soccer Science tore into Tottenham, never allowing Klinsmann and company to get into their elegant stride. And as they powered forward, so Everton scored the goals that were to win the tie and take them on to Wembley.

Despite the fact that they were without the suspended Duncan Ferguson, the Blues were in no mood to settle for a draw. The scoring spree began when Matt Jackson (standing in for the Cup-tied Earl Barrett) got into the act; then Graham Stuart made it 2-0 before Spurs pulled one back through a dubious spot-kick which Klinsmann converted. Joe Royle decided the time had come to send on his Nigerian international, Daniel Amokachi, who had been more out than in the side since his £3 million move from the Continent. And as Spurs pushed players forward in their efforts to snatch an equaliser, they left gaps at the back which the speedy Amokachi exploited to the full. Twice he broke through, and twice he beat keeper Ian Walker, who had already defied several scoring efforts. Amokachi went close to hitting a hat-trick as Everton ran out 4-1 winners. For Spurs, there was no way back, and so the dream final remained just a dream.

Manchester United's route to Wembley had been by way of conquests over Sheffield United (a third-round victory by 2-0 at Bramall Lane), a 5-2 Old Trafford romp against gallant Wrexham (who had had the temerity to score first), then the 3-1 demolition job on Leeds United and another home victory (2-0 over Queen's Park Rangers) before meeting up with Crystal Palace and emerging 2-0 winners in a Villa Park replay, after the first encounter had produced a 2-2 draw. The respective managers, Alex Ferguson and Alan Smith, had appealed for peace before the tie, after a Palace fan had lost his life following the first semi-final meeting. However, football suffered once more during the replay when Roy Keane was seen to stamp on Palace captain Gareth Southgate and, for his sins, he received a three-match suspension (plus a fine). Keane, who made a public apology for having committed his offence, was able to play in the final along with Paul Ince, though Eric Cantona was merely a spectator. Ryan Giggs was on the bench, with Andrei Kanchelskis missing after a hernia operation.

By this time, Manchester United had seen Blackburn Rovers clinch the Championship. So the FA Cup was by way of being a consolation prize for United . . . or was it? That became the crucial question as the match at Wembley got under way, with Duncan Ferguson, like Giggs, sitting it out at the start. Both Giggs and Ferguson were about to make their comebacks after injury, while Amokachi, the semi-final hero for Everton, was also on the substitutes' bench as Joe Royle gave his vote to Paul Rideout and Graham Stuart, with Anders Limpar aiming to provide a good service from the wing. In fact, once play had got under way, it was United who threatened to uphold their reputation and their standing as favourites, but Everton showed that they were ready to slug it out, even as they were forced on to the defensive. Gradually, they began to push forward themselves – and that was when Manchester United came unstuck, as their defence was unlocked by a swift counter-attack.

Limpar collected the ball in his own half after Ince had lost possession; he took the ball forward then released a pass into the path of the overlapping Jackson, who delivered a perfect cross behind the United defenders. There was Stuart, in the right spot to strike for goal – but when his shot struck the bar, it seemed Everton's chance had been blown. However, as the ball bounced out, Rideout was waiting, and he rammed a header home, leaving Schmeichel stranded and the helpless Steve Bruce – victim of a hamstring injury – unable to get to the ball.

Bruce was an absentee at the restart, and Giggs appeared on the left to try to galvanise United into scoring action. He certainly injected life into United's attacks, although Mark Hughes had been held in a vice-like grip by the Everton defence, with David Unsworth rock-solid and skipper Dave Watson an inspiration in the middle of the back-four line. Everton's counter was to pull off Limpar, who was feeling the effects of an injury, and send on Ferguson and then Amokachi, as United drove forward time and time again. Before the end, in fact, Schmeichel was up inside Everton's penalty area, so desperate were United to snatch the goal that would give them another chance in extra time.

If Watson was indomitable at the heart of Everton's defence (he won the TV Man of the Match award), Neville Southall came into his own with four super saves – one effort tipped over the bar, another snatched to safety and the others a double-barrelled save which foiled substitute Paul Scholes when he seemed a certain scorer.

As time ticked away and Everton defended resolutely, aided by some good fortune, it became apparent to the fans of both sides whose day this was going to be. Towards the end, the Everton faithful were in full cry, while the United contingent for the most part stood mute and looking miserable, as if they realised that the game was up and their heroes would finish with nothing for their efforts throughout a long and difficult season. That was how it proved, so Everton went up for the Cup and United had to settle for being second-best again, so soon after their failure to prevent Blackburn Rovers from claiming the title.

In the space of eight days, indeed, United had seen Kenny Dalglish's team hailed as champions at Anfield, of all places – and this after they had lost 2-1 to Liverpool. Added to this was the knowledge that Liverpool themselves had claimed the Coca-Cola Cup, and so United were the odd ones out as the north celebrated the winning of three trophies. It was a bitter pill for Ferguson and his players to swallow, but he was gracious enough to compliment Joe Royle on Everton's success.

Ferguson and Royle, in fact, had forged a friendship quite a while before that final, when Joe was the manager of Oldham and Ferguson was in charge of the Scotland international side. Royle had contacted Ferguson then to put forward the name of Andy Goram as a potential international goalkeeper and, of course, Goram nailed down the job as Scotland's last line of defence. Ferguson did say he felt his players had deserved to get some reward for their efforts during season 1994-95, but the neutrals certainly believed that it was fair the honours should go round again, after United's domination of the domestic scene for a couple of years.

For match-winner Rideout, the end of the season produced yet another challenge, but it was one he awaited with confidence, knowing that his self-belief had grown. Under Howard Kendall and Mike Walker, Rideout had flitted in and out of the first team at Goodison Park; then the arrival of Joe Royle had seen his fortunes improve, as the new manager paired him with Duncan Ferguson. At the age of 30, Rideout had just about seen it all since he had kicked off with Swindon Town and joined Aston Villa, before his travels had taken him into Italian football, with Bari. Then it was back home, to Southampton, Swindon Town (on loan, this time), Notts County and Glasgow Rangers. At £500,000, he had been a player Everton could just about afford in Howard Kendall's day, although his career at Goodison Park could hardly be said to have flourished. Yet he had tried to retain his self-belief, never forgetting that on the first occasion he played in front of a national audience (at Wembley, 15 years previously) he had struck a hat-trick in a Schoolboy international.

Rideout knew as well as anyone that in football things can change overnight, and he was well aware that with the arrival of Peter Johnson there was cash in the kitty for reinforcements – indeed, Joe Royle was already reckoned to be foremost in the bidding for Nottingham Forest's Stan Collymore, whose price-tag turned out to be a record £8.5 million. Rideout, whose goal had ensured Everton's first trophy in eight years and taken them into Europe, was still prepared to sign up for another three years at Goodison Park, despite the potential threat from at least one front-line newcomer. 'I know the club have got the money and are looking for new players; but whether Collymore comes or not, I want to stay. The boss has been up-front with me; he has offered me a three-year contract, and with the squad we have and the manager ready to strengthen it, I don't see why we can't challenge for more honours.' For Rideout, that winning goal was something special, because it meant that he had maintained his record at Wembley: 'I scored in each of my three appearances there for the Schoolboys, and the goal against United was my 16th of the season, my best record in the top flight.' So the player who had been signed from Rangers almost in desperation had repaid the £500,000 fee, first by scoring the goal (at Ipswich) that guaranteed

Everton's stay in the top flight, and then by hitting the winner in the FA Cup final. Oddly enough, he had seen Mo Johnston precede him south from Ibrox Park (and be labelled a £1.5 million misfit), then he had watched Duncan Ferguson follow him from Rangers.

If skipper Dave Watson won the television pundits' award, it was the 36-year-old Southall who claimed the Bobby Moore trophy after his goalkeeping heroics. But the veteran goalkeeper declined to join in the after-match banquet celebrations. Instead, he went home to Llandudno with his family after talking about the kind of attitude which had helped Everton to achieve their success. Southall said: 'We think we're a pub team. That's the way our mentality is. We will go anywhere and give anybody a game. I suppose we're similar to Wimbledon, really; but we can play when given the chance. We went into the final with the pub-team attitude that it doesn't matter who we play – we're going to have a go. If it doesn't work out, it doesn't work out; but everyone came off that Wembley pitch dripping with sweat, having given everything they had. It's the same right through, from the management to the lads who didn't play. The spirit and determination to do well after the disastrous start to the season has made us a better team.'

Southall, in fact, was the sole survivor from Everton's previous campaign in Europe, the Cup-Winners Cup triumph of 1985, shortly before the tragedy of Heysel brought about a ban on English clubs. He reflected that 'according to everybody else before the final, Manchester United should have won. It was the same with Spurs before the semi-final. Why should we give a damn? They're the same as us – two arms, two legs. In some departments they might be better than us, but they have to show the same will, the same desire. I think we showed the greater desire on the day.' It was a verdict with which few people would disagree.

Southall, the one-time binman who graduated to top-class football via the non-League route, looked ahead to another European campaign, saying: 'It would be good to win again; it would be nice if I left Goodison as a winner.' The goalkeeper's career first took off when Bury spotted him when he was playing in non-League football; they signed him for £6,000 from Winsford Athletic and he turned out to be a bargain buy – when he joined Everton, the Goodison club forked out £150,000, and they had tremendous value for their money, as well. International honours came his way, as well as Championship and Cup medals, but it wasn't all plain sailing, especially during season 1994-95. Indeed, Southall himself admitted that in the early days of the season, he had begun to dread the arrival of the morning post, which contained hate mail on more than one occasion.

If he had been virtually an ever-present since his arrival 14 years earlier, he was now being blamed in some measure for Everton's shocking start to the campaign, and with the increasing pressure on him, the keeper was stung into verbal retaliation as he exchanged angry words with a fan behind his goal, then made what was regarded as an offensive gesture. This brought Southall a postbag of hate mail, including a letter in which the writer threatened to burn down the player's house. Southall was all for chucking the letter in the bin, but Mike Walker, his manager at the time, regarded the threat as being serious enough to bring in the police. Fortunately, however, no more was heard about the matter and, of course, as the season progressed and Everton went to Wembley, Southall regained the affection of the fans and emerged as a hero.

Southall declared that 'proving people wrong doesn't bother me; all I do is go out and do my best. I'm not really interested in what people say – if the manager picks me, well and good. If he doesn't think I'm playing well enough for selection, that's life.' One of his former managers, Howard Kendall, commented in a piece in Southall's testimonial brochure: 'I feel Neville's frustrations in his career have been when he believed Everton FC were not good enough to challenge the best.' Southall himself clearly believed he could meet the challenge not only of playing for Everton but of managing Wales, although he and Mike Walker were among those who saw the job go to Bobby Gould.

As for Everton and his future there, he made it plain he intended to carry on as before, even though he would have reached the age of 37 by the start of the new season. During the summer of 1995, he trained harder than for some years, and as he looked ahead he echoed the comments of Kendall as he talked about Everton. 'When you are at a massive club like this, you should be doing better than we have. Of course, it is frustrating. But I am certain we are on the right lines, and I have nothing but praise for the way the club has tackled its responsibilities over the past few months. I look forward to being part of the success which I feel is coming to Everton.'

At that stage of his career he had totalled 650 appearances in Everton's first team – 494 of them League games – and collected 81 international caps. And if he had felt frustrated by Everton's past failings, he declared his belief, also, that the Welsh set-up 'needs a damn good shake-up, from youth level to the top. I am sick of being an international loser – I want to be a winner.' So Bobby Gould, the new incumbent, could be in no doubt about the ambitions of Wales's last line of defence, who reckoned that 'over the next five years we could have the best group of players we have ever had – I believe we are good enough to qualify for the finals of the top international tournaments.' Under Gould, who named Southall and Ian Rush as coaches, Wales won their next match, against Moldova. But only time would tell . . .

Meanwhile, Neville Southall could look back with great satisfaction upon one footballing occasion: the testimonial match against Celtic which, in the summer of 1995, drew more than 21,000 people to Goodison Park and, it was estimated, made Everton's goalkeeper the richer by some

£200,000. Southall made a couple of brilliant saves as the match ended in a 2-2 draw. If he had chosen to dispense with joining in the FA Cup final celebrations a few months earlier, the Goodison Park occasion was a personal tribute to a player who, over the years, had been regarded by Everton's supporters mostly as a hero. Even if, at times, he had appeared to be somewhat eccentric, a fellow who preferred to go his own way.

Southall, described by one critic as 'a quirky fellow', explained his decision to travel home, rather than join his team-mates in their Wembley celebrations: 'I'm not a person for big celebrations. I hope the lads enjoy their night. We came here to do a job, and we've done it. Now I'm going home.' And so he joined his wife, Eryl, and their daughter, Samantha, before leaving with the words of his manager ringing in his ears: 'Neville's nicely awkward, but as long as he keeps playing like that, I don't care. When I took this job, fingers were being pointed at him; but he's been magnificent. He's a strong-willed character with an abrasive sense of humour. I let him get on with it. He didn't want to know about the banquet. I asked him to stay, and he said, "Why?".'

And so, as the team left London for their open-topped bus triumphal return to Merseyside on the Sunday after the final, and up to 300,000 people turned out to welcome them, it was said that 'If the blue half of Wembley felt the vaguest stab of sympathy for the red half of Manchester, then they concealed it pretty successfully. The truth is that Evertonians can scarcely believe the way things have turned out. Back in the bleak midwinter they couldn't have found Wembley with a road map. Endsleigh was their destination, despair their prevailing emotion. Came November, came Joseph of the Broad Shoulders, and out came the sun. The League deficiencies were swiftly remedied, the confidence came gushing back and, suddenly, everything was possible.'

There was a reminder that it was a Swedish international, Anders Limpar, who had set the Wembley ball rolling for

Everton, and not just with the perceptive forward pass which launched his team-mates on to the golden goal: 'George Graham cursed him at Arsenal. Mike Walker did the same at Goodison; but Royle loosened the reins and his instinct was rewarded.' Royle, it was said, had 'pulled a master-stroke', also, by naming the team which had pulverised Tottenham Hotspur in the semi-final. 'Resisting the temptation to play Duncan Ferguson from the start and keeping him chained with Daniel Amokachi to the bench, the manager rewarded those who brought Everton to their season's crescendo.'

Yet, even as Joe Royle enjoyed the sensation of being a winner at Wembley, 'his thoughts were turning to what might become of Everton in the seasons to come when, he hopes, he never has to hear the word "survival" again'. And so Everton and their manager made the most of a tremendous emotional occasion on 20 May 1995 while looking ahead to a future filled with more hope than they would have dared to expect, back in the gloomy days of November. It could so easily have been a Vale of Tears, instead of the Cup that Cheers.

Chapter Fourteen

THE FERGUSON FILE

All in the space of less than a week, Everton's £4 million striker, Duncan Ferguson, had walked up the steps of the royal box at Wembley to collect an FA Cup-winner's medal from His Royal Highness Prince Charles, and been taken down to the cells below Glasgow Sheriff Court after having been sentenced to three months in jail, becoming the first professional footballer to have received a custodial sentence for an offence committed on the field of play.

Before the court's sentence had been passed, the player's father had passed a comment that 'it is because of who he is and who he plays for that this case has come to court'. At the time of the offence, Duncan was a Rangers player. And while Everton Football Club made it clear that they were 'fully supportive' of Ferguson, when he made his court appearance, after sentence had been passed another voice was raised – this one in solemn warning about the way that things were going in what Pelé had once termed 'the beautiful game'. Gordon Taylor, chief executive of the Professional Footballers Association (who had spoken out in defence of Eric Cantona), called for the courts to return disciplinary powers to the soccer authorities. Whether or not his call fell upon deaf ears remains to be seen.

Ferguson had arrived, along with Ian Durrant, on loan from Rangers during the time that Mike Walker was in charge at Everton, and it is fair to say that the striker had come down from Scotland with something of a reputation. On the one hand, he was readily regarded as a footballer of great ability; on the other, he had been known to 'use the heid', as they say in Scotland, and thus upset opponents. His appearance at Glasgow Sheriff Court in May 1995 concerned an alleged, on-the-field assault upon another player, John McStay, when Rangers played Raith Rovers. The incident was seen on television, and while Ferguson claimed it was an accidental clash of heads, Sheriff Alexander Eccles saw things in a different light.

Ferguson, then still only 23, was reminded by Sheriff Eccles that he had been found guilty of a serious offence which constituted 'totally unacceptable behaviour', although 'on this occasion I accept that it took place in the background of a highly charged football match, a contact sport involving a certain amount of violence. However, it was not in the course of play, but during a stoppage – and, in my view, a clearly deliberate act.' This was not the first time Ferguson had been involved in a violent clash, said Sheriff Eccles, 'and in the public interest, and to bring it home to yourself that such behaviour cannot be tolerated from a footballer who is in a prominent position and whom younger people look up to, I impose a sentence of three months'.

Naturally, the defence counsel, Donald Findlay QC, had pleaded for the player, and there had been a presentation of background reports, although Sheriff Eccles made it clear that he viewed community service (such as had been imposed upon Cantona) as the easy option. Ferguson was released on bail, pending the result of his appeal against conviction and sentence, which was due to be heard in Edinburgh in October 1995. An appeal had also gone in against the 12-match ban imposed by the Scottish Football Association, which meant that the player would be free to kick off with Everton at the start of season 1995-96.

Meanwhile, south of the border, Gordon Taylor was

chipping in with the way he saw things: 'This is starting to take things into the absurd. Football should be capable of dealing with these things. What is becoming apparent is that with high-profile players, the authorities are not happy to let football deal with them. That's a worrying trend. Duncan Ferguson got a 12-match ban from the Scottish FA for this incident and it was then put on the back-burner. Now it's gone one for more than 12 months. Eric Cantona, I felt, was appropriately dealt with by his own club, but then it was added to by the FA and then by the courts.

'If we are not careful, we will be having penalties for high-profile stars coming from every direction. You just worry that people are losing a sense of proportion. I don't condone what Duncan did, but John McStay didn't complain about it and didn't want any action taken by the police. Yet this has gone before the courts, and Duncan has received a custodial sentence. It is clearly a worry.'

It was clearly a worry for Everton Football Club, too. The 12-match spell of suspension by the SFA had been carried over to his career with the Goodison club, though it had been left hanging in the air pending that appeal.

While Ferguson's transfer from Rangers had gone through, Durrant had returned to Scotland within a relatively short space of time; even, in fact, before Joe Royle took over as Everton's manager. As for Ferguson, he had come a long way in a short time during what could be described as a colourful and controversial career. And there was an interesting background to the story, because it concerned not only Ferguson and Rangers, but also Jim McLean, the chairman of Dundee United after a 21-year spell as manager of the Tannadice Park club.

It was recorded that in 1975 Dundee United had made one of their very rare mistakes – they had allowed striker Andy Gray to cross the border and join Aston Villa for no more than £110,000. Gray eventually became a hero to the Everton fans, and it was said that as he achieved outstanding success at club and international level, Dundee United and their manager vowed that never again would other clubs profit from such bargain buys. Then they discovered Duncan Ferguson, and as he progressed to the point where he had claimed four Scotland caps before he was 20, so he attracted the attention of other clubs. Rangers, for one, expressed keen interest; Leeds United, for another; and along came Everton, managed by Howard Kendall, to declare their interest as well. Dundee United were rated as certain to transfer young Ferguson to Leeds, for £3.25 million, when Everton stuck their oar in.

In the event, the player went to neither of these clubs. When he did finally arrive at Ibrox, the transfer fee had escalated to the point where it reached £3.75 million while his wages, it was said, had risen from a reported £300 to £5,000 a week. Thus Rangers were obliged to fork out what was then a British record fee for a player who, according to striker Ally McCoist (no mean marksman himself), had cost over the odds. McCoist had gone on record as saying that 'everybody knows Rangers paid too much'. Rangers manager Walter Smith, aware of Ferguson's reputation, said on his arrival at Ibrox: 'His record is there and everybody knows about it; so I can't guarantee that he won't have his moments.' Smith saw Ferguson 'as a natural progression from Mark Hateley – we've had a lot of success from that style of player, and I hope it continues along the same lines'.

Too much money or not, Ferguson, with typical confidence, expressed the view that Rangers would get their money's worth; and while his career at Ibrox lasted from the summer of 1993 to the later months of 1994, Everton did shell out to make him their own. While McCoist felt that Rangers had paid too much for Ferguson, he also believed he had the potential to become one of the finest strikers British football had ever seen. As was pointed out after he had joined Everton, he wasn't merely a handful when it came to aerial duels – he could play football on the ground as well.

By the end of 1994 Joe Royle had the job of channelling the player's skill and energies along the right lines, just as he had the job of dealing with other players at Goodison such as Daniel Amokachi, Vinny Samways, Paul Rideout, Matthew Jackson and Neville Southall.

FA Cup-final hero Southall's viewpoint on Joe Royle and on former manager Mike Walker was interesting, as he talked about people having written him off. On Walker: 'I thought as a fellow he was different class – and he was okay as a manager. But it's other people's decisions, and I had divided loyalties.' Southall added: 'At the same time, a lot of people were writing me off. That's life. People have their opinions. I don't care.' Then, he said, Joe Royle came in, 'and it was up to me to prove that I was needed'.

When Royle arrived, Everton had taken eight points from 14 matches (including only one victory); by FA Cup-final day they had lost only half a dozen games out of 34 played. It was said that Southall was considered to be beyond his sell-by date when Royle arrived at the club. The talk at Goodison was of a replacement – in fact, two names were being mentioned during the months leading up to the FA Cup final. One was Paul Gerrard, the England Under-21 keeper Royle had groomed and left behind at Oldham; the other was Rangers' Scotland international, Andy Goram, whom Royle had also groomed.

So Southall stayed, and no one arrived to challenge him for his place. Royle, who declared that he had gone to Goodison with an open mind, admitted that 'I had seen one or two goals go in on television, and people were pointing the finger at Neville'. He added: 'We had a couple of interesting days between us – things were crackling about a bit and then, from the first game, he was magnificent. I can honestly say he's not cost us a goal since I've been here. If you ask him about his performance [at Wembley] he will be very unassuming about it. He's his own man, and you just let him get on with it. As long as he keeps playing like that, I'm not bothered.'

Royle paid Southall this compliment: 'On current form, I have not seen a better goalkeeper in the Premiership.' And Southall returned the compliment: 'I have the boss to thank for everything. He showed he had faith in me; he gave me back my self-belief.' While Southall was able to reflect that his Goodison Park career had indeed taken an upward turn, several other players were left wondering what the future held for them – Amokachi, Jackson, Samways and, possibly, Graham Stuart and Stuart Barlow among them.

One player who knew for certain that his days had been numbered at Everton was full-back David Burrows, who has been on a real merry-go-round of the clubs during recent seasons. Burrows had been signed for Liverpool by Kenny Dalglish, at a fee of half a million pounds, and when he left West Brom, he had told me: 'My career at The Hawthorns had gone downhill. I'd played in the first team, dropped back into the reserves and seemed to be getting nowhere.' The man who restored his belief in himself was Nobby Stiles, then coaching at West Brom. 'He told me I was still a good player; he gave me every encouragement to persevere.' The result was that Dalglish signed him. Then, during the Graeme Souness era, Burrows was shunted off to West Ham, along with Mike Marsh, in a £2 million exchange deal which saw Julian Dicks going to Anfield. Dicks returned to Upton Park not many months after having left the Hammers; Burrows moved on again, this time back to Merseyside, but with Everton. And after Joe Royle had arrived, he was on the move once more, to play for Coventry City and Ron Atkinson. His transfer value had doubled to £1 million – which helped to offset Everton's £1.7 million outlay on Earl Barrett, whom Atkinson had signed from Joe Royle's Oldham for Aston Villa. So the wheel of soccer fortune turns.

Vinny Samways had been a £2.2 million capture from Tottenham Hotspur, but he hadn't exactly raised the temperature during the time Mike Walker played him in Everton's first team. By the time the FA Cup final came around, Samways was up for sale, clearly having failed to convince Joe Royle that he was needed for the senior side. As for Amokachi, Jackson, Stuart and Barlow, there appeared to be question marks against the names of at least three of these, especially with Duncan Ferguson and Paul Rideout rated the favourites for the front line, and talk of massive bids for Stan Collymore and Dennis Bergkamp. Amokachi and Jackson, certainly, were left wondering if their Wembley feelgood factor would last.

Royle had expressed his admiration for Duncan Ferguson's ability, and he had noted how swiftly the Everton faithful had taken to the Scottish striker. He seemed confident of his own ability to handle Ferguson as well. Royle had also offered Paul Rideout a three-year contract, and the 30-year-old Wembley match-winner had expressed his determination to stay and fight for a place, no matter whom the manager signed. But for Amokachi, the two-goal hero of the semi-final triumph over Spurs, and for Jackson, the match-winner against Bristol City in the fourth-round tie at Ashton Gate, there was that feeling of uncertainty. Amokachi had been in and out of the side over the previous months and, indeed, at one stage he had been reported as almost desperate to get away from Goodison; it was even suggested that he had issued a plea for a Continental club to 'come and rescue me'.

Jackson, like David Burrows, had seen Earl Barrett arrive as a £1.7 million reinforcement, and while he was clearly on a high, like Amokachi and Graham Stuart after Everton's triumph at Wembley, he was also realistic as he admitted: 'My only thought was to wonder if it was my last game for Everton. I've been offered a new contract and I want to sign it, but I have to be realistic . . . I want first-team football.' Obviously, he considered that Barrett hadn't been brought in to play reserve-team football. He would surely have been in

Everton's FA Cup-final line-up, had he not been Cup-tied. As for Amokachi, he, too, admitted: 'I don't know if I'll be staying. That's something only the boss can decide.'

The transfer talk was fuelled by reports that Everton chairman Peter Johnson had been in contact with Massimo Moratti, the multi-millionaire boss of Inter Milan, proposing a deal for Dutch World Cup striker Dennis Bergkamp (who, as it turned out, became an Arsenal player at £5.5 million), while Everton's pursuit of Stan Collymore was well publicised. So, whichever way you looked at it, Everton were in the market for a big-money signing up front. Meanwhile, the financial columns were not slow to pick up on a story about the chairman of the Goodison Park club, although there appeared to be some rather contradictory quotes.

It was reported that Johnson's Christmas-hamper group, Park Foods, was up for grabs – the suggestion then being that Johnson was keen to find a 'friendly' but hungry buyer for his 65 per cent controlling stake. This, apparently, was in order that 'he can concentrate all his time on his new love, Everton Football Club'. The story went on to relate how the man it described as 'the King of the Toffeemen' was 'over the moon' when Everton defeated FA Cup favourites Manchester United. Johnson, it was further recorded, having taken over at Goodison Park in July 1994, 'has committed around £10 million of his own cash to buy players, but his spending is unlikely to stop there'.

The report described how Peter Johnson had founded Park Foods 27 years previously 'and has masterminded its heady progress'. According to the story, 'last year its agents, who collect weekly subscriptions from retail customers, supplied 1.5 million hampers to 1.25 million homes'. Results 'due soon [this was in May 1995] should see pre-tax profits rise from last year's £11.8 million to £14.7 million. Johnson now apparently wants to sell out so that he can spend more time supporting the Toffees. Shareholders could be in for an early Christmas present if a buyer is found soon.'

Immediately after this report, there was another story saying this time that after NEC had decided to end its long-term sponsorship deal with Everton, it was being hinted that the Goodison outfit would find new sponsors in . . . Park Foods. It seemed as if you paid your money and you took your choice. But there was more to come, because only a few weeks later there was yet another version, which declared: 'Nothing gets up Park Foods Group chairman Peter Johnson's nose more than suggestions that he might sell out to spend more time at Everton Football Club, where he owns 50 per cent.'

And hard on the heels of that statement was a quote from Peter Johnson himself: 'Clubs are not run the same way as businesses. I am a non-executive director there. It is a hobby. Park Foods is not for sale. I am keeping my eye on the ball.' So were Danka, who became Everton's new sponsors.

Two things had become indisputably certain: that Everton's fortunes had altered dramatically with their FA Cup triumph and their impending excursion into European competition; and that manager Joe Royle's hand would be strengthened when it came to investing in the transfer market and competing on level terms with the likes of Manchester United and Liverpool, not to mention Newcastle United, Arsenal, Aston Villa, Blackburn Rovers and anyone else who cared to delve into the top end of the player market.

Commercial director Clifford Finch was able to confirm the feelgood factor when he declared: 'The difference between a fortnight ago, when we were scrapping – though I never once believed we would go down – and now is incalculable. It's very big bucks. I would say the difference to the club between winning the FA Cup and not winning it is millions of pounds.' The sponsorship by NEC had lasted for a decade, and it had ended when its logo was carried on the players' shirts for the last time, at Wembley. Finch declared: 'I expect a hot-line, because I think a number of companies held off to see not only what we did in the Cup, but whether we stayed in the Premiership.' That, of course, would be no more than prudent for would-be investors in a football club. Big business wants to be involved with those who are winners, not losers. As the late Harry Reynolds, one-time chairman of Leeds United, used to say: 'You get nowt for being second.'

'We're an international attraction now. I would think the next three-year contract we sign would bring something like £2 million to the club. It would be a considerable increase over what we have been receiving.' There was the prospect of a new kit contract, too. 'The one with Umbro ends next May. We are right in the middle of negotiations for a contract that will take us from 1996 to 2000. Umbro are still in there pitching, but they are one of something like seven manufacturers who want Everton's business.' Income was expected to rise, too, with progress in the European Cup-Winners Cup; and the gates had already shown a healthy increase, with attendances in the Premiership campaign having reached an average of 32,000. All in all, Joe Royle could reflect that from now on, 'shopping at Harrods', as he put it, would be a vastly different proposition from the days when he had to wheel his trolley round the bargain basement as he went shopping for Oldham. But, as he well knew, he had to extract full value for every penny he spent, no matter whether it was £10,000 or £10 million.

According to one sportswriter, there had been a shift of power, with the success during season 1994–95 of Liverpool, Blackburn Rovers and Everton: 'A football uprising is building up to a deafening drumbeat in the ears of Manchester United.' It was recorded how, at Wembley, 'a giant awakened from slumber: Everton are back'. As Alex Ferguson admitted, after his club's heady years of triumph: 'Sometimes players can forget what defeat is like. They know now. This is the first time in five years we've won nothing.'

It was recorded that 'with bountiful transfer cash pledged

by chairman Peter Johnson, it seems there will be many more exciting days ahead for Everton and the remarkable Joe Royle'. As Everton's manager himself said: 'We have just moved into a different market. There are too many top-class players who have gone to other clubs without Everton being too interested. But now we can be interested in the best.'

Yet Royle didn't forget the men who had done the job for him. He declared: 'We are not going to buy willy-nilly. We have a good squad of players, and they deserve first crack at it. They've been terrific. You just have to look at the record since I came for proof of that – six defeats in 34 games is European form on its own, without winning the Cup.'

Chapter Fifteen

IF YOU CAN'T STAND THE HEAT . . .

One by one, like Cabinet Ministers summoned to pledge their support for the Prime Minister, various chairmen of clubs in the Premiership delivered their own verdict in the summer of 1995. Arsenal's Peter Hill-Wood, Tottenham Hotspur's Alan Sugar, Aston Villa's Doug Ellis – they followed a growing trend in the top echelons of football as they spoke out against spiralling transfer fees, even as their own clubs shelled out small fortunes on new players. Peter Swales had told me several years earlier: 'The time is coming when clubs will put a ceiling on transfer fees – there's a growing feeling that this escalation can't be allowed to go on.'

The sports editor of the *Daily Mail*, Vic Robbie, wrote a tongue-in-cheek article at the time Manchester United were transferring Paul Ince to Inter Milan, but he wasn't joking when he made this assessment, at the beginning of the piece: 'In a summer of mercenary madness, football clubs are outbidding each other in an orgy of inflation as they send transfer fees escalating into the realms of indecency. Even players unable to establish themselves in the national team are moving for mega-millions with personal terms that make the Gas Board chairman seem like a pauper.' Well, Arsenal's chairman denied that Dennis Bergkamp, who had cost £5.5 million, would be getting £20,000 a week – 'That's slightly exaggerated,' he said.

What Peter Hill-Wood also said was this: 'The transfer market has gone absolutely mad. Other clubs do it, and we have to stay up there with them. It's crazy. I said that 20 years ago, and it's getting crazier. We are competing for the top players, and will continue to do so. We will find the money for new signings.' Arsenal's outlay on Bergkamp was more than double their previous record fee (£2.5 million to Luton Town for John Hartson), and Hill-Wood said: 'I thought £5 million for Chris Sutton was a lot of money, just as I thought £80,000 for Frank McLintock was a lot when we paid that to Leicester in the 1960s. But, as then, we have a responsibility to our supporters to stay in the game and pay these prices.'

Manchester United manager Alex Ferguson had described the £5 million fee Blackburn Rovers paid to Norwich City for Chris Sutton as 'madness'. Then Ferguson himself did a deal with Newcastle United which amounted to £7 million, as Andy Cole moved to Old Trafford and Keith Gillespie (valued at £1 million) joined the Magpies, with Newcastle manager Kevin Keegan – having angered the Cole devotees on Tyneside – declaring that time would tell which club had profited most from the transfer.

Tottenham's chairman, Alan Sugar, having agreed to pay Crystal Palace £4.5 million for Chris Armstrong, then launched what was described as 'a fierce broadside on the irresponsible spending of England's Premier clubs'. Sugar had just put his name to a club-record cheque to sign Armstrong saying: 'It's difficult for clubs like ourselves to compete in the market place when irresponsible amounts of money are being paid which make no sense in the respect of a company's balance sheet.'

Aston Villa's chairman, Doug Ellis, had seen his club thwarted in bids for various players but, having seemingly missed out on Les Ferdinand, Bergkamp and Stan Collymore, Villa finally managed to land Crystal Palace skipper Gareth Southgate. It cost the Midlands club their record fee – £2.5 million. Then their chairman declared: 'The sums being spent on fees and wages now seem stupid; but they say that if you can't stand the heat get out of the kitchen – and I'm not getting out of the kitchen. I'm going to compete.' A few days later, Villa were spending even more – £3.5 million on a Yugoslav international striker.

Bob Paisley once told me that he didn't believe the day would dawn when transfer fees went through the £2 million barrier. He lived to see sums of money far in excess of that figure change hands. Bob was still the manager of Liverpool when he offered his opinion, and he had raised a few eyebrows himself when, in the summer of 1977, he went to Scotland and paid Celtic £440,000 of Liverpool's money for Kenny Dalglish – after having first sold off Kevin Keegan to Sport Verein Hamburg for a cool half million. By the summer of 1995, Liverpool themselves were locked in a battle with Everton, the idea being to sign striker Stan Collymore from Nottingham Forest. It was a battle in which each club was prepared to shell out no less than a British-record fee of £8.5 million. And when the deal was done (or seemingly done), what a furore there was, because Forest themselves were declaring that unless Collymore agreed to sign a waiver form and forfeit his claim for £425,000 of the transfer fee, he would be compelled to remain at the City Ground. Manager Frank Clark's argument: 'It states in his contract at Forest, which still has two years to run, that he would be entitled to 5 per cent of the fee if sold at our behest. We have done everything in our power to keep him – the final words to Collymore from our chairman were that we would match any financial offer made to him by Liverpool or any other club. We will not move an inch on this issue.'

Collymore, remember, had still to make his mark at international level, even if he had managed an appearance in an international jersey. And some months before the striker had been put up for sale by the reluctant Clark, Alex Ferguson had gone way past the £5 million Chris Sutton fee to land Andy Cole – another striker whose appearance on the international scene had been fleeting, as season 1995–96 loomed. Manchester United's fans were not amused when their club did an about-turn and agreed to sell Paul Ince and Mark Hughes, but it could not be denied that, financially, this was good business from the Old Trafford club's point of view. They had had excellent service from both players, had made a huge profit on Ince and almost got their money back on Hughes. His chairman, Martin Edwards, dismissed claims that the cost of building a new £28 million stand had forced a policy of panic selling.

Ironically, while Manchester United missed out on the championship and the FA Cup in season 1994–95, Newcastle missed out not only on both these targets, but upon qualification for Europe in 1995–96. Would they have qualified, had they kept King Cole? Would Manchester United have retained the FA Cup, had Cole not been Cup-tied? No one can answer those questions, of course . . . Just as no one can say for certain if any club can even hope, let alone expect, to recoup an £8.5 million fee paid for a footballer. Which brings us back to Liverpool, Everton and Stan Collymore. Joe Royle may have talked about 'shopping at Harrods' but, like his Liverpool counterpart, Roy Evans, he knows he's expected to get value for money. After all, during a dozen years at Oldham this was an almost daily chore.

One might wonder if Liverpool had some misgivings about shelling out such a massive fee for Collymore – and not merely because it set a new British record. Whether or not Everton lost out with their failure to land the striker from Forest remains to be seen. When I put it to Everton's manager that a fee of £8.5 million was one which could never be recovered, he was quick to tell me: 'Everyone thought the first £100,000 transfer fee was outrageous, and that such a state of affairs couldn't be allowed to continue – but look what happened over the years. If a club has got the money to splash out, then that club will spend it – and carry on spending it.' And Joe Royle echoed the words of Newcastle United chairman Sir John Hall when he said: 'Now that we've seen a player go for £8.5 million, it won't be long before some club is thinking about forking out £10 million. Maybe Liverpool didn't really want to pay out all that money – come to that, neither did we; but it was the going rate, the price you had to pay if you wanted Stan Collymore.'

Royle almost landed the striker from Nottingham Forest, too – in the final analysis, he was led to believe that it was Collymore's friendship with several of the Liverpool players, notably Jamie Redknapp, which swung the deal Liverpool's way, a view confirmed by Frank Clark. Certainly there was no ill-feeling on Royle's part about the striker having opted for Anfield. As he told me: 'We always had more than one player in our sights. To be perfectly honest, had we paid all that money for just one man, it might have stopped other things from happening during the summer.' According to one report, Everton had been prepared to offer Collymore wages of £15,000 a week and a contract extending for four years – terms which, it was said, were considerably better than those on offer by Liverpool. Right to the death, Everton were reckoned to be favourites for the 24-year-old striker, but in the end they accepted that they had lost out. 'We're disappointed, but nothing more than that,' was how Joe Royle put it. 'As I understand it, it came down to the personal thing of him knowing several of their lads. We wish him luck.'

The importance of the deal was reflected in the fact that, despite the jetlag immediately after his return from Australia, Royle had plunged straight into the negotiations with the player, while Liverpool manager Roy Evans had interrupted a Caribbean holiday to fly back and join chief executive Peter Robinson in discussions with Collymore and his agent at an hotel near Heathrow airport. After three hours of talks, Evans flew back to St Lucia, completing a round trip of 8,500 miles.

There was a revealing comment from Liverpool's chief executive after they had clinched the deal for Collymore. Peter Robinson admitted that his club's return to the European arena had influenced the decision to pay such a staggering amount of money for a player who, at one stage of his career, had appeared to be going nowhere in particular. Rejected by Walsall as a teenager and having failed to impress Wolves sufficiently, Collymore had faded into the non-League backwater as he joined Stafford Rangers. And even after Crystal Palace had resurrected his career at League level, it seemed as if he might well not scale the heights, as he travelled on to Southend. But in July 1993, Nottingham Forest took a £2 million gamble when they signed him. Peter Robinson said: 'Two things swayed the deal; he is young, and he is English. He has the potential to be a top player for a long period. The fact that Stan is English put a premium on the price because of the restrictions which limit the number of foreign players you can use in European competition.'

No doubt such considerations exercised the mind of Joe Royle, too, as he immediately set in train another sequence of events; this time he talked to Collymore's old club, Crystal Palace, about striker Chris Armstrong, while also being linked with Aston Villa's Dean Saunders and Leeds United's Brian Deane. Once again, Everton's manager knew that he faced competition for Armstrong because Tottenham Hotspur were in the hunt, after the departure of Jurgen Klinsmann. Once again, then, there was the prospect of a tug-of-war, and once again, the player made his choice. The pull of staying in London proved too strong, and Spurs became Armstrong's destination. Had Everton succeeded in persuading him to join them, they would have been taking much less of a gamble than Liverpool, in financial terms, although when I discussed this aspect with Joe Royle, he said, with a shrug of the shoulders: 'It's part of the job, when you're a manager. And, like any other manager, I've taken a few gambles in my time. When I was at Oldham, for instance, I was always having to take my chances in the transfer market, both as a buyer and a seller. And I knew I had to try to make every penny count.' By mid-September 1995, a Belgian player named Jean-Marc Bosman had caused Everton and every other club to think long and hard about what might happen to the transfer market.

When I talked to Joe's wife, Jan, on one occasion, about her husband's early days in management, she told me: 'The first couple of years were the worst.' That, of course, was when he was still a fledgling team boss at Oldham. And when I asked Joe himself about the hard times, he told me: 'I didn't really think about quitting the job, but the second season at Oldham was the worst. We were really struggling, coming towards the end of the season. We had sold several players and raked in around half a million pounds. John Ryan, Paul Atkinson, Paul Futcher, Rodger Wylde – they had all gone for varying fees, to bring money in, and I had also brought in four replacements at a total cost of £70,000. There were only two or three games to go to the end of the season, and it was a very worrying time as we fought to stay up; but we managed it in the end, and I was a very relieved man. From then on, we were able to make genuine progress, even though at times it was a matter of taking two steps forward and then one step back.'

One of the things which, people claimed, helped Oldham to scrape through and achieve some surprising results was the fact that they were playing on an artificial surface at Boundary Park. Some folk labelled the pitch Oldham's 'plastic paradise'. At least one manager, to my certain knowledge, had difficulty in getting his own players to believe they could perform on that Boundary Park pitch – it was, said the manager, a 'psychological barrier' which his players had to surmount, and when he tried to get this through to them, he couldn't do it. No matter how much he talked to them during the days before they played at

Oldham, once they went out, their thoughts were centred on how to combat the pitch as much as how to combat the opposition. In the event, they took a hammering.

Joe Royle always refuted the notion that Oldham's 'plastic paradise' gave them the edge, and that they themselves suffered when called upon to play on real grass at other venues. Managers like Kenny Dalglish and Howard Kendall expressed their dislike of playing on artificial turf, but their teams had to do it at Oldham, Luton and elsewhere. Oldham did demonstrate that they could get results away from home, although at times they went for fairly lengthy periods without a win. Yet they survived.

There has long been a genuine friendship between Joe Royle and Alex Ferguson, yet this does not disguise the keen rivalry whenever their teams meet, and at one stage during the 1995 FA Cup final Royle was seen to leap to his feet and call out: 'Hey! What's going on here?' Clearly, he had witnessed some incident or refereeing decision which he felt should not have happened. Looking back, Everton's manager recalled 'one of my greatest moments when I was the manager at Boundary Park' – the day Oldham Athletic took on Manchester United at Maine Road, in the semi-final of the FA Cup. 'I always felt that this was one of our finest displays, not least because of the qualifications people had expressed about our ability – or so-called lack of ability – to perform on grass like we performed on our own artificial pitch. We took United on, and we gave them a really hard time of it as we shared half a dozen goals. Their keeper, Jim Leighton, was outstanding for them, while Paul Ince in midfield held them together there.' What Joe Royle didn't say, but what his players were unanimous in claiming afterwards, was that Oldham felt some of the Manchester United players 'got away with it' when it came to 'rabbiting on' at the referee. They reckoned some of their opponents did an excessive amount of talking out on the pitch, without being told to 'put a sock in it'. Not that Royle or his players expressed any kind of grudge against the opposition or the referee; and it is indeed unusual for Everton's manager to start shouting the odds.

But he did take exception, and said as much, when Everton played Newcastle United at St James's Park towards the end of season 1994–95. In fact, Royle's remarks appeared to have put him in danger of falling foul of football's authorities although, ultimately, no action was taken. During that match, which Everton lost 2–0, referee David Elleray decided to show the red card to Earl Barrett and Barry Horne, as well as booking no fewer than five other Everton players. Royle condemned Elleray's handling of things as 'the most insensitive display of refereeing I have seen in 30 years'. And he was given backing by his chairman, Peter Johnson, who declared: 'I'm sorry to have to say this, but we now have a major referee problem, and I don't think I'm alone in believing this. Standards are slipping, and we should really consider inviting ex-professionals to train as referees. Referees are becoming the new stars – and that cannot be right.'

It has to be said that the opportunities are there for former professional footballers to become referees; it also has to be said that, these days, referees in the Premiership are paid what most people would consider to be a handsome amount of money for doing what is, for them, a part-time job. David Elleray, for example, was a schoolmaster at Harrow when he officiated at the Newcastle-Everton match. And he had his say afterwards, too: 'Overall, relationships between players and referees this season are better than ever before. But it seems that scapegoats are always needed in football, and referees are the easiest targets. Everybody else takes their turn at being a winner or loser, but we can never win.'

Everton's manager accepts that you win some, you lose some; and he accepts that for all the brilliant buying he has done through a dozen years and more, he has still made the odd mistake. One player who cost Oldham Athletic £750,000 – striker Ian Olney, signed from Aston Villa – proved to be an expensive investment indeed, because by the start of season 1995–96 he had still to demonstrate that he would pay off that fee. Admittedly, much of the problem had been caused not through the player's own fault. And another costly signing, Neil McDonald – who arrived at Boundary Park from Everton in a £500,000 transfer deal – ended up by being written off and given a free.

When Joe Royle talked about the signing of Neil McDonald, he had this to say: 'We all make mistakes, and perhaps the McDonald business was the biggest I made during my dozen years at Oldham. He was brought in because I believed that he would add quality to the team; but, for various reasons, things just didn't work out. For one thing, I felt that there was a problem when it came to his fitness, though there were other factors.' Everton had signed McDonald from Newcastle United for half a million pounds, and when they sold him on to Oldham, they got their money back. He could play at full-back or in midfield and, according to a member of the backroom staff at Boundary Park, he was the best passer of a ball at the club. But his career went backwards, rather than forwards, and finally Joe Royle decided that the time had come for a parting of the ways, even if it meant letting the player go on a free transfer – which, for a club like Oldham, was no small matter when it came to going from £500,000 to a free.

When I asked Joe if, looking back, there was one thing he might well have changed, he pondered for a few moments, then admitted: 'Perhaps, after we had stayed up at the end of our second season in the top flight, I should have moved on then. It was a case of not being able to spend the kind of cash required to bring in new faces – and perhaps a new face on the managerial side might have helped the club. But it was a great club, and it didn't seem to matter that I'd been there such a long time. And having seen Howard Kendall, Colin

Harvey, Howard again and then Mike Walker manage Everton in turn, that seemed to be it. It appeared to me as if Everton, having stuck to former players so many times in the past – remember, before Howard and Colin, and going back in time, there had been Harry Catterick and Billy Bingham – had decided to break the chain and go for someone who had no previous connections with the club. The appointment of Mike Walker seemed to me to be a kind of statement by Everton, a decision to break away from keeping the job in the family, so to speak. So far as I was concerned, they had had the chance to come and get me, had they wanted to do so. Maybe it had never been quite the right time . . . Who knows? But in my own mind, Everton were always the one club to persuade me to leave Boundary Park; and when the chance finally did come, I had no hesitation. In fact, I took the job even before I had worked out the terms of a contract at Goodison. Overnight, I was being introduced as Everton's new manager, and the deed was done.'

So Joe Royle took the job the moment it was offered, and it changed the course of his career – and his thinking when it came to investing in the transfer market. He had no qualms about forking out £4 million for Duncan Ferguson; and he didn't feel he had to play footballers who had cost huge sums of money and were already on the books. Daniel Amokachi and Vinny Samways, for instance, had been signed for a total of more than £5 million, but they found that under their new boss they could not count on regular first-team places. After his failure to land Stan Collymore and Chris Armstrong, Royle decided to bide his time. In any event, he had other posers to solve, such as the refusal of Matt Jackson and Gary Ablett (signed from Liverpool for £750,000 in January 1992) to accept the terms offered as their contracts came to an end. These Cup-final heroes, as Joe Royle admitted, were two of the players he did want to keep at Goodison Park.

If the Neil McDonald deal ended in disappointment, the

transfer involving another player with Oldham-Everton links turned out to be perhaps the shrewdest stroke of business Joe Royle did, considering that the player concerned had been home-grown. Royle transferred Mike Milligan to Everton for £925,000, bought him back for £600,000 – then sold him on to Norwich City for £750,000. So the net profit to Oldham was more than £1 million – and Oldham had several years of tremendous service from the player.

Gambling in football? Joe Royle has taken a few risks, but when we talked he revealed: 'Possibly the biggest gamble I took was not when it came to forking out a hefty transfer fee, but in making a decision which could affect the way a crucial game went. I'm referring to the first leg of Oldham's semi-final tie against West Ham, in the Littlewoods Cup, when we were drawn to play at home. I reckon that we would have given AC Milan a game on that artificial pitch, and when West Ham arrived to play there I had a hunch that they would decide to use a sweeper. So before the Oldham players went out, I told Ian Marshall to keep a sharp eye on Willie Donachie, our coach, and if West Ham did line up with a sweeper, to watch for Willie's signal.

'I'd decided that while Marshy could do an effective job at centre-half, we could benefit from pushing him up front straightaway, and that's just what we did. The gamble paid off handsomely, too, because Marshall caused the Hammers' defence all kinds of problems, and by half-time we'd rattled in three goals. During the interval I had a rethink, and I told Marshy to drop back to his normal centre-half spot, so he reverted to this role as the second half got under way. We went straight out and scored a fourth goal, then knocked in another couple more, and ended up winning the match 6–0. We needed some kind of insurance, too – when we played the return game at Upton Park, West Ham, who had nothing to lose, came out looking for goals and they went three up. But that was the end of the scoring, so we came through and went to Wembley.'

If Joe Royle took a gamble for that semi-final contest, he took an even greater gamble in leaving the security of his job at Boundary Park for the somewhat dubious prospect of pulling Everton round in a matter of a few months. But he told me firmly: 'I never look back, and while it was a bit of a wrench to leave Oldham after so long, I could really have no regrets. They had been very loyal to me for a dozen years, and they had given me my start in football management. I left Goodison Park as a player on Christmas Eve 1974 after some tremendously happy years there, and in all honesty I cannot claim that I felt destined to return one day as Everton's manager. Yes, there was a time when it seemed as if I was in with a chance of something bigger – not just at Everton, but elsewhere. I turned down Manchester City because, for one thing, the timing wasn't right, and there was talk about West Ham and Sunderland, although no approach was ever made to me about the Roker Park job. When it came to Everton, I had been led to believe that I was in contention, but when Howard Kendall went back to Goodison for the second time, I stopped even thinking about it. Then, when it happened, it all came so suddenly it took me by surprise.'

By the start of season 1995–96, Joe Royle had just reached the age of 46, which offered the prospect of plenty more years as a team boss, and plenty more years of pressure in a high-profile job. He could remember how Kenny Dalglish had quit at Liverpool (and in June 1995 he moved 'upstairs' at Blackburn); he could go back more than two decades and remember how his first manager, Harry Catterick, had bowed out at Everton in the summer of 1973. 'I think that at that time ill-health had begun to take its toll,' Joe reflected. When I put it to him that in his own case, Everton might well turn out to be his final job in club management, I half-expected him to agree straightaway. But, with a shrug and a smile, Joe Royle gave his answer in a couple of words: 'Who knows?'

Well, he was on the shortlist for the England job once; and he has since been in charge of England Under-21 sides, so he has gained some experience of what working at international level entails. Maybe, just maybe, there will be another opportunity for him to test himself; this time in what Peter Swales called 'the most difficult job of all'. Remember, the call finally did come for him to return to Everton – and he's still young enough to follow in the footsteps of Terry Venables. Yes, indeed . . . Who knows?

Chapter Sixteen

RUSSIAN ROULETTE

The sizzling summer of 1995 was one of discontent for Manchester United manager Alex Ferguson and United's fans. They lost Paul Ince, Mark Hughes (and almost Eric Cantona), while in the case of Ukrainian winger Andrei Kanchelskis, United did an astonishing *volte face* twice over and, in the process, found their friendly relationship with Everton being put under considerable strain. In the case of the errant Frenchman, Cantona, it was recorded that he had made it clear he had changed his mind and decided to stay at Old Trafford only because of manager Ferguson; in the case of Kanchelskis, it was recorded that 'Andrei loves the club, the players and the fans, but he cannot work with the manager'. Thus spoke his agent, Grigory Esaylenko.

A furious Ferguson was stung to respond: 'If Andrei says he can't get on with the manager, that's fine. But that's not the issue. He signed a new contract last year for five years – that's the important issue.' And a final sting in the tail: 'I'll see Andrei at the start of next season.' But Ferguson didn't, and neither did Manchester United – because, despite having been ordered to report back for training with the Old Trafford outfit, the Ukrainian, having ostensibly been sold to Everton, declined to return down the East Lancashire road to United's training headquarters. And so the saga of his on-off transfer continued, with talk of Everton making an issue of it in the High Court and United reportedly boycotting a tribunal.

Oddly enough, even as United and Everton remained involved in this tug-of-war over the winger, Joe Royle was springing to the defence of his United counterpart on another matter – one which concerned a newspaper phone-in as to whether or not Ferguson should remain in his job. The newspaper reported that slightly more than half the 800-odd people quizzed had delivered the verdict that Ferguson should go – to which he replied dismissively: 'City fans, calling in and making mischief. They'd love to see the back of me, wouldn't they? Well, they'll have a long time to wait – a bloody long time.'

While wishing Everton good luck after having wrested the FA Cup from Manchester United, Ferguson didn't flatter them; and he upset some of their fans when he declared: 'I still can't believe we really lost that Cup final. I mean, you never like getting beaten by an ordinary team. Then you remember the way your own team played and you think, "If they were ordinary, what does that make us?"' What, indeed? However, Ferguson was granted the Royle seal of approval when it came to the newspaper poll, which Everton's manager termed 'a disgrace to journalism'. Royle declared: 'Alex knows what he is doing. You don't achieve what he has done by not being good at your job.'

Big Joe was good enough to take his team to Wembley, there to see off Blackburn Rovers and add the Charity Shield to the FA Cup which stood on the Everton sideboard. It wasn't a great game, and it didn't alter the fact that match-winner Vinny Samways was still up for sale, if he wanted to leave Everton, but it was a hopeful pipe-opener to the real thing, as season 1995–96 kicked off the following Saturday.

In the meantime, the Kanchelskis question still required an answer – notably, whether Everton would not only get to keep him, but whether they would be given an extension of the deadline, that he would qualify to play for them in the

European Cup-Winners Cup. The Kanchelskis saga had dragged on for weeks, with the winger initially apparently having suggested that if he were granted his wish to shake the dust of Old Trafford from his feet, the club of his choice would be Rangers. Then it was reported that, should he be listed, he would jump at the chance to join his former United team-mate, Bryan Robson, who had just steered Middlesbrough into the Premiership. 'The race for his signature is between Everton and Middlesbrough,' it was reported. 'Even though they have not yet recruited his replacement, the Old Trafford hierarchy believe he must go. A top-level meeting at Old Trafford between chairman Martin Edwards, Alex Ferguson, Kanchelskis and his agent reviewed the whole transfer scenario. The player emphasised his determination to get away . . . it was decided the situation had become intolerable and that the player should be sold immediately. The Merseysiders are confident they will win the battle, and were negotiating with Kanchelskis last night. Joe Royle, frustrated this summer at missing out on Stan Collymore and Chris Armstrong, is determined to grab Kanchelskis. Royle's initiative will be backed by the financial clout of millionaire chairman Peter Johnson.'

Middlesbrough's main hope rested on Andrei's relationship with Robson: 'The Russian international has a regard for Robson bordering on reverence from their playing days together at Old Trafford.' So what happened next? Right at the death, it seemed, there came an intervention from a third party (big-spending Arsenal), but this last-ditch bid to hijack the £5 million move to Everton ended in failure. Even Bryan Robson, a close friend and confidant during a sometimes turbulent career at Manchester United, could not sway things. Kanchelskis, when the crunch came, opted for Everton.

Joe Royle revealed: 'When I first asked Alex Ferguson about him at the end of last season, I didn't have much hope;

but as the summer wore on, signs became better. I knew that Andrei had an inkling for this club, but the danger was Bryan Robson – they had an affinity, and Robbo is a charismatic figure. Andrei will have our fans on the edge of their seats every time he gets the ball. He's the best right-winger in the English game – no question about that.' Royle, who had only just paid Derby County £2.6 million for centre-back Craig Short, had now spent £13 million overall during his nine months at Everton in what was termed 'his vigorous plan to turn the FA Cup winners into Championship contenders'.

Little did Everton's manager realise, at that stage, that he and his club would have to endure some anxious moments before they could finally claim that Andrei Kanchelskis was their own. Right there and then, Joe Royle was happily reflecting: 'It's a strange feeling for me . . . in a dozen years at Oldham I probably spent £3 million in all. I recall signing Mark Ward for £7,500; £5 million is a world away.'

As for Kanchelskis: 'Manchester United treated me very well. I don't want to talk about the past – I'm looking to the future. I hope to be part of Everton's success. I'll try to play as well as I did for United, maybe better. I can further my career at this great club. Their FA Cup win said much about the manager and his ability to get the best from players.'

Everton chairman Peter Johnson had something to say about the new recruit as well: 'Our fans tell me they think Kanchelskis is a better buy than Collymore would have been.' He added: 'The days when you could always expect to get a seat here are over.'

Yet there remained one or two surprises along the way for club and player. Kanchelskis, for instance, was made aware that if Manchester United had treated him well, Everton were not prepared to match the Old Trafford club in certain aspects – yet, astonishingly, they were more than prepared to accommodate him in other ways. Meanwhile, Alex Ferguson was summing up on why he had finally done an about-turn over the winger: 'I just felt it was a situation that was going to fester. We had to listen to a diatribe from his agent at the last meeting. You say to yourself, "What is the point? Andrei doesn't want to play here." You realise you have just to get on with your life and look forward to next season with players who want to play for the club. I could never understand the personality issue that Andrei spoke about, but the best thing now is to lay it all to bed. I think we made the right decision to get it over and done with.' But it wasn't 'all over and done with' . . . not by a long way.

Big-spending Everton, it was reported, had a shock for their £5 million recruit, because perks were out: 'At Manchester United, Andrei had a house and a car. He doesn't have that with us. We don't give houses and cars to players. We feel today's players are paid good salaries and bonuses, and should buy their own,' said Everton's commercial director, Clifford Finch. Sentiments which would be echoed by many others in and out of football. 'It's a trap we don't want to get into. We are trying to take the club forward, both commercially and on the pitch [Everton, in fact, wore the logo of their new sponsors, Danka, for the Charity Shield outing at Wembley]. We can't do that if we are spending our time with estate agents and car dealers.' So Kanchelskis knew the score there. He had words for the Old Trafford faithful as well; 'I hope they will forgive me for signing for Everton. They were always very supportive, and I hope they understand my situation. I am not one who looks for trouble, and I am not moaning about anything. I had great enjoyment at United, but it is time to make a fresh start.'

But if the news on the housing and motoring front was not to his advantage, it was much, much better in another direction, because Andrei was reported to be receiving a massive £1.2 million pay-off in signing for Everton. This remarkable figure, it was said, arose from a clause in his contract with United, and it thus took the total paid for his transfer from Old Trafford to £6.2 million. According to the report, United insisted that they should get £5 million from the deal, and so Everton 'agreed to cover any contractual obligations owed to the player by paying the extra money'. What Everton were not prepared for – and what they were not prepared to do – was shell out another £1 million when the Ukrainian's former Russian club, Donetsk, demanded a cut of the deal. Everton secretary Mike Dunford, having confirmed that United would receive £5 million, declined to confirm also the amount Kanchelskis would receive. 'Personal terms remain confidential,' he said. But it was reported that Kanchelskis was entitled to 30 per cent of the profit from the transfer to Everton. 'The clause may explain why clubs like Tottenham and Middlesbrough pulled out of the chase for Kanchelskis, claiming the price was too high. But Everton were prepared to meet the demands after missing out on Collymore and Armstrong,' ran the report.

When the Donetsk demands were made, the Kanchelskis transfer appeared to be up in the air, as Manchester United sensationally called off the deal and ordered the player to report back at Old Trafford. This development came ten days after the transfer had seemingly gone through – but, apparently, there had been a week of discussions behind the scenes. 'There is no problem involving United or Everton,' it was said. 'The complication arose as a result of inquiries made by Kanchelskis's previous club in Russia.' Donetsk were believed to be wanting a £1 million-plus slice of the transfer fee, 'contrary to the impression given to the two English clubs'. Alex Ferguson said: 'It is a complicated matter, but the upshot is that Andrei will be back with us on Monday.' That certainly didn't happen, but the argument about the deal dragged on. 'As far as we are concerned, the deal is dead. If we can have him back, I would be happy to welcome him into our first-team squad.' Thus spoke Ferguson, as Kanchelskis still awaited his debut for Everton (he had missed a warm-up game at Oldham because of what were termed 'transfer technicalities', and he was to miss the Goodison meeting with PSV Eindhoven). By the time the

Charity Shield match was being played, he still hadn't worn an Everton jersey in match action – that weekend he was away with the Russian international side, while the dispute over his move from United was still unresolved. And the big kick-off was mere days away. Everton, it was said, were 'losing a race against time to register Kanchelskis for their European Cup-Winners Cup campaign' – if he were not registered by the Tuesday, he would be ineligible for the opening two rounds of the competition. Indeed, he would still be eligible to play for Manchester United in the UEFA Cup! And by then, the talk was of arbitration.

If people wondered how Kanchelskis would fare because of his refusal to return to Old Trafford, Everton chairman Peter Johnson spelled it out: 'Andrei will remain at Everton.' United solicitor Maurice Watkins spoke of 'continuing dialogue' with Everton, but claimed: 'Kanchelskis has never stopped being a United player, and the deal was always subject to contract.' By then, 18 days had passed since the Ukrainian had 'joined' Everton.

From Everton's chairman came this claim: 'We entered into full and final agreement for the purchase of Kanchelskis with the board of Manchester United. While Everton sympathise with their predicament [the claim from Donetsk], we expect United to honour their agreement. Andrei will remain here, and we will continue to assist United in resolving this problem.' Yet, after what were said to have been '48 hours of fruitless talks between the clubs', Everton called in the Premiership. Then came the accusation that United were breaking their word, as Clifford Finch criticised United's U-turn over the deal. Insisting that terms for the transfer had been agreed with Old Trafford chief executive Martin Edwards on 20 July, Finch said: 'You can't have two chairmen agreeing a deal, then, seven days later, one of them saying that it's not enough money. We have already spent £20 million, and we don't have a bottomless pit of money that anyone can take advantage of.'

By that time, Everton fans were becoming restless, as they recalled the last-minute collapse of a move to Goodison for Brazilian striker Muller during the Mike Walker era; and, plainly, the breakdown of the Kanchelskis deal was the last thing the expectant supporters wanted. Clifford Finch revealed that Everton had 'gone a long way down the road to try and find a compromise . . . these sort of deals have been struck between chairmen since football began. When chairmen agree terms, to all intents and purposes it should be binding.' As for Kanchelskis, he remained defiant. 'I've had no contact with United and I will not go back there. I am staying at Everton.' It was reported that even an offer of extra cash from the Goodison club had failed to end the sorry saga – which was why Everton, insisting that any sell-on clause was solely the concern of United, had called in the League. Finch revealed: 'Everton have, at all times, agreed to Manchester United's conditions up to the point of the chairmen of both clubs agreeing to the transfer on 20 July. On 27 July, United informed Everton of a new development, and it is this that has formed the basis of the dispute between the two clubs. In spite of Everton's additional financial offer of a compromise, it appears no solution can be found. Therefore, Everton have no alternative than to refer the dispute to the Premier League for arbitration.'

The amazing saga continued with a report that both Everton and United planned to list Kanchelskis as their player for European competition when the UEFA deadline arose – 'but it is United who still hold his registration'. As for the League arbitration tribunal, 'United have failed even to name a nominee for the panel'. It was said that in another move, 'Everton have appealed to the FA to invoke Rule 41, which allows them to arbitrate and reach a binding decision without the clubs' consent'.

Joe Royle had not become involved in the arguments over the transfer of Kanchelskis, but there was a ray of hope as it became known that Donetsk were ready to negotiate on their claim for cash from United. And yet: 'We are entitled to a percentage; we really want it and we really need it.' This was on the eve of the Charity Shield game, just before the scheduled Premier League arbitration panel's meeting – which United had refused to attend on the grounds that it was 'not appropriate'. Then came news that Maurice Watkins, United's solicitor, had flown to the Ukraine in a bid to break the deadlock. Forty-eight hours to the UEFA deadline . . . and less than a week to the start of the season.

On deadline day, Everton had become resigned to being unable to register Kanchelskis for the Cup-Winners Cup – and by then, Clifford Finch had returned to the attack. Hours after it was reported that Maurice Watkins was returning from the Ukraine with the situation still in deadlock, so far as Donetsk was concerned, Everton's commercial director delivered a stinging rebuke to Manchester United as he charged them with having adopted a 'selfish' attitude. He said: 'It is deplorable that a contract United have entered into with a third party creates a liability to Everton. It should not be allowed to frustrate a legally binding agreement entered into by the two club chairmen. People may say, why don't we pay the £1.14 million to Donetsk? But we should not have to be held to ransom.' Finch further declared: 'I call on United, for the sake of football, the player and the supporters to take the honourable course and agree to Andrei's release. He has stated publicly that he will not return to Manchester United. All he wants to do is pull on an Everton shirt.'

But while the Football Association had supported Everton's claim to have the European midnight deadline extended, in view of what were considered to be special circumstances, UEFA made it clear a player could be registered with only one club – so, since United still held the registration of Kanchelskis, he would be seen as their player. The Football Association had also asked United to agree to arbitration but, according to Finch, 'it is a slow process . . .

we have been told it could take four to six weeks to resolve'. And he argued: 'We really need someone to grasp the nettle and sort it out – United could resolve it tomorrow.'

One question nobody appeared to have asked so far – publicly, at any rate – was this: when United signed Kanchelskis from Donetsk, was there a clause in the contract about Donetsk receiving a sell-on cut? If so, United should have known about it all along, and it should not have cropped up as a matter of dispute involving Everton a week after the winger's transfer to the Goodison club had been agreed. If United had forgotten or ignored such a clause, that was no fault of Everton either. If United had known the clause was there and had not wanted to fork out more than £1 million to Donetsk, the sell-on cut should have been added to the transfer fee in the first place, with Everton's knowledge and agreement . . . or the deal should have been called off then. At that stage, then, it seemed valid to ask if United had slipped up over the Donetsk clause when agreeing the deal with Everton, just as it seemed logical to argue that, unless United had made it clear to Everton at the outset that they would be expected to contribute some or all of the money due to Donetsk, then Everton could fairly claim that theirs was not the responsibility. Even then, some folk might have argued that Manchester United, unfortunate though they were, might well have been satisfied to make a handsome profit from selling Kanchelskis, despite the demand from Donetsk; especially since, apparently, Everton had already agreed to take on the burden of paying the player his massive cut from the deal.

Admittedly, United had never wanted to let Kanchelskis go in the first place, but they had come to the conclusion that there was no longer any point in holding him. And the day after the European deadline had passed brought startling news of another twist. In the morning, it was reported that United had changed their minds and decided to ask the Premier League to settle the transfer dispute. 'Kanchelskis looks certain to miss Everton's opening game of the season and may well be absent for the FA Cup-holders' first appearance at Goodison next Wednesday.' It was said that 'Everton angrily rejected a proposal from United that the two clubs and Kanchelskis each pay a third of the money demanded by Donetsk', and Clifford Finch was quoted thus: 'I was astonished at the suggestion, and turned it down flat. I have found some of the events over the last few days unbelievable in many ways and distasteful in others. Andrei is very upset. We are the injured party – the only people suffering are Everton, Andrei and our supporters.'

It was reported also: 'The frustrating period of inactivity Kanchelskis must endure can only be determined by the speed with which the Premier League can set up their arbitration panel. Ironically, a commission was in place for Monday, but United refused to attend. At the time, Maurice Watkins was in the Ukraine, attempting to reach an agreement with Kanchelskis's old club.' The United hierarchy now accept that the only sensible route forward will be for the Premier League to resolve the dispute. The parties concerned have to accept that the decision of the commission is binding.' This, then, appeared to be the situation – and the probable way out of the impasse – just three days before the big kick-off. And as the outlook at last appeared hopeful for Everton, there was good and bad news on other fronts, with defender Matt Jackson indicating he was ready to sign on again for three years, after a move to Sheffield Wednesday had fallen through; and it seemed that even an offer of £1.3 million had not been sufficient to persuade Oldham Athletic to part with England Under-21 goalkeeper Paul Gerrard.

But a matter of hours after the report that Manchester United were now prepared to go to arbitration, Everton were being angered by the announcement that the Old Trafford club had called off the Kanchelskis deal and demanded his return. United were said to want to clear £5 million on any deal involving the player. 'The issue still seems likely to be decided either by a Premier League arbitration council – or in court.'

For United, Maurice Watkins confirmed: 'Everton have referred the matter to arbitration. We have a letter from the Football Association informing us of this, and we're considering our position. I want to stress that we have been working very hard to resolve this matter.' And as Martin Edwards announced that 'negotiations with Everton for the transfer of Kanchelskis have been called off', he revealed just what had happened concerning the demand by Donetsk: 'Original negotiations proceeded after a fax was received by United from Donetsk, procured by a representative of the player and signed apparently by a vice-president of Donetsk, waiving their rights to 30 per cent of any transfer fee above the monies already paid to them. On the basis of the above waiver the player negotiated his terms with Everton. United subsequently received a further fax from Donetsk, this time signed apparently by the president of Donetsk maintaining the club's claim to the 30 per cent payment. The effect of this demand would be to reduce the net payment to Manchester United by £1.14 million. Under these circumstances, we have been forced to withdraw from negotiations with Everton.'

Joe Royle, maintaining a low profile, declined to say anything, but Clifford Finch declared: 'United are members of the FA and should play by the rules of the association. They can make as many statements as they wish, but all they are doing now is confusing Andrei. It is now a human problem. Andrei is going to be back from international duty not knowing where his future lies. There will be no more money; only the £5 million that has been available from day one.' The ball, clearly, had been bounced back into Manchester United's court, and it remained to be seen if other interested parties – Arsenal and Middlesbrough, for instance, who had both been in the running for Kanchelskis's signature – would reappear on the scene. Or, possibly, Blackburn Rovers.

In the meantime, the manager of the current champions was giving Everton and Joe Royle a massive vote of confidence. Ray Harford, who had in previous seasons tipped Arsenal and Leeds for success (which both clubs had achieved), came out strongly as a backer of Everton in the race for the title. He named them 'a good outside bet', and explained: 'I say that because of their mentality. You have to want to be strong to start with, in the Premiership. The English game is based on being hard to beat and then concentrating on winning. I look at Joe Royle's team, now he's got a player in over the summer [Craig Short], look at the way they finished last season, and they do appear a threat.'

Harford reflected upon the previous term and said: 'During the first few months Joe was there, they looked fearsome. When we played them at Goodison Park we somehow won – but we got absolutely battered. I think Everton will be up there with the best this season.' Well, that remained to be seen . . . yet, as the Kanchelskis affair rumbled on, it was crystal clear that with the flying winger in their side, Everton would be even more difficult to beat than before. Apart from any question of his relationship with Manchester United's manager, it was easy to understand why Kanchelskis would be upset if his move to Goodison Park were scuppered – it was reported that the four-year deal he had agreed with Everton would be worth £2 million to him. If so, that wasn't bad for someone who, at one stage of his career, was said to have been playing for no more than £6 a week. Kanchelskis was praised as a great signing for Everton, a player who could transform the team, but he was also told that 'there are no get-out clauses in his contract, because we don't like them. He is here for four years.' There were also words of warning from Gordon Taylor, chief executive of the Professional Footballers Association – directed not at

Everton, but at the way the game generally was going. Taylor, talking about spiralling transfer fees and players' wages, declared: 'The danger is that if the market collapses, some clubs will face financial insolvency.' (At that stage Jean-Marc Bosman had not yet successfully challenged the legality of the system whereby a club can demand a transfer fee for a player whose contract has expired.)

Right there and then, Everton were facing the collapse of the deal with Manchester United, and as each day passed it seemed to bring more confusion. A Football Association spokesman was quoted as saying that they now appeared to have no part to play in the proceedings, while Everton were said to be holding a crisis meeting of their legal team. And with the return of Kanchelskis it was reported: 'He will defy Manchester United and train with Everton . . . he flew in from international duty determined that the arrival lounge of Manchester airport was the closest he would get to Old Trafford.' Kanchelskis declared: 'I don't know what is going to happen, but I am training with Everton tomorrow – that is for certain.'

It was reported: 'United, who are still paying his salary, will expect Kanchelskis to report no later than Monday – or risk being fined or even suspended. But when his dream move was first thrown into doubt, the unhappy player confided to friends that he would strike, rather than return to United. He not only ignored Ferguson's demand then that he return to train; he moved his family out of their club house.'

Ferguson declared that 'the bottom line is that he's paid to play football. He must not get involved in all the politics.' And the Professional Footballers Association was said to be concerned, and anxious to avoid 'any strike scenario'. Ironically, it was reported, 'Everton's own generosity of spirit led to their downfall – they paraded Kanchelskis on 21 July, but agreed to delay the completion until 1 August, to suit United's financial year. Donetsk made their £1.14 million demand on 27 July, scuppering the deal.' So Everton 'continue to pin their hopes of resurrecting the deal on arbitration and, in a statement, claimed 'Both clubs have agreed, through membership of the FA, to submit all differences to arbitration in accordance with procedures laid down by the FA. This will now lead to an arbitration hearing. This has been confirmed by the FA.' And FA spokesman Mike Parry confirmed that this indeed was the case . . . but 'no one at United was available for comment'. So the whistle still hadn't been blown on the game of football that had turned into Russian roulette.

Everton returned from their first-leg match with Reykjavik on the right end of a 3–2 scoreline, but by then Kanchelskis was out of action for weeks after having sustained a shoulder injury while playing against Manchester United at Goodison (where United managed a 3–2 win). Everton had deserved at least a point from their display against United. Joe Royle also wanted more from the European return than he had seen during the game in Iceland.

Veteran keeper Neville Southall spelled out a warning to his team-mates as he celebrated both his 37th birthday and his 500th League appearance for Everton: 'We have kidded the rest of the Premiership into believing we are a good team. We won the FA Cup and staved off the threat of relegation, and suddenly people were saying we were back at the top, suggesting we had turned the corner. It would be fatal if the players started to think that way. Short-term success can hide so many flaws, and we must be very wary.' On comparisons between the current Everton and the Howard Kendall-inspired team which conquered at home and in Europe, Southall declared: 'We're still a fair way from matching the quality of the squad Howard pulled together. That was a fabulous team, one that probably never got the credit it deserved. People should remember that it took Howard three or four years to get it right – Joe Royle hasn't even had 12 months yet. We must now make sure we make progress each and every season. This time around we're back in Europe, and that must be our primary objective every August, because this club needs that sort of platform upon which to perform.'